LIQUID
HEALTH

OVER 100 JUICE AND SMOOTHIE RECIPES
INCLUDING PALEO, RAW, VEGAN, AND GLUTEN-FREE

LIQUID HEALTH

LISA MONTGOMERY

Hatherleigh Press is committed to preserving and protecting the natural resources of the earth. Environmentally responsible and sustainable practices are embraced within the company's mission statement.

Visit us at www.hatherleighpress.com and register online for free offers, discounts, special events, and more.

Liquid Health

Library of Congress Cataloging-in-Publication Data is available.

ISBN: 978-1-57826-577-0

Cover and Interior Design by Carolyn Kasper

Printed in the United States

10 9 8 7 6 5 4 3 2 1

www.hatherleighpress.com

Contents

Dedication

*L*iquid Health is dedicated in loving memory to Mr. Richard "Dick" D. Powell (September 19, 1934–June 14, 2014).

In early 2007, I went to SCORE (Service Corps of Retired Executives) in Pottstown, Pennsylvania for help in promoting my first wellness expo—"The Raw 50 Wellness Expo," which would feature Carol Alt, as well as Donny Good who was battling health challenges at the time. We were honored that both Carol and Donny had decided to share their stories with us, but I needed help spreading the word of how changing their diet had transformed their lives. Ironically (and/or divinely) SCORE assigned me Mr. Henry Pollock, a retired executive and the former president of one of my former customers. He took one look at my request and sent me straight to Dick Powell.

Dick was a retired teacher and had been a local TV personality for many years. Dick was energetic, supportive, and always helpful. Together with the assistance of his lovely wife Lucille, the two of them helped me promote the expo and turn it into a success. We had countless TV spots, as well as consistent radio and newspaper coverage. We were relentless in getting the word out. Years later, people continue to be astounded at the vast coverage we managed on what would otherwise be considered a small town event. And if it weren't for Dick, none of it would have been possible. He supported me through the ups and downs of trying to put together the expo. He was there for the tears, the frustrations, and the joys of the expo.

We are blessed in life by the many people who come to our aid. Both Dick and Lucille stood alongside me, loved me and supported me through not only the journey to the expo, but all the years since.

Both Dick and Lucille have been like surrogate parents to me. I couldn't love them any more than I already do, even if they had been my own Mom and Dad.

Dick, this one's for *you*!

Introduction

 *"To* life!"

When people get together to celebrate the big events in their lives—weddings, holidays, graduations—they toast the event. The toast, "To life!" made famous by the musical *Fiddler on the Roof,* has always resonated with me. I decided that *Liquid Health* would be an expansion on that toast. In *Liquid Health,* my goal is that you raise your glass, not just to "life," but to a life lived healthily and dynamically. *Liquid Health* is a tool to help support and educate you, enabling you to live a healthier lifestyle.

But people's lives are very busy nowadays; even when we try to slow down, our lives speed right back up again. That's why *Liquid Health* makes it easy—it shows you that *anyone* can throw healthy ingredients into high-speed blender or run them through a juicer. You don't have to be a neurosurgeon or a rocket scientist to use this book. You may not have time to make a seven-layer raw salad, but you absolutely have time to throw some genuinely healthy ingredients in a blender and push the button.

When you're going through life's challenges, or when you're starting to feel tired and rundown, know that it's easier on your body to digest liquids. It takes less energy and time. We never really think about it, but the challenges of life can be so overwhelming at times that the physical act of digesting food—even healthy food—seems like too much to handle. *Liquid Health* is the gentle and easy way for you and your body to get the nutrients your body needs.

Liquid Health is full of amazing, delicious recipes that are not only healthy, but also easy to make. While I was putting together this collection, the thought at the forefront of my mind was that each person is an individual. What works for your body may not work for the next person's body.

With that in mind, each recipe is marked as belonging to one of more of the following diets: raw (R), paleo (P), gluten-free (GF), or vegan (V). I've also included a brief explanation on each of these recipes, for those curious about expanding their palate. This also makes it easy for those already following these lifestyles to locate the recipes that suit their needs. I have also noted places where a recipe can be rendered usable with another diet simply by changing an ingredient or two. For example, removing raw honey from a recipe and replacing it with stevia will render the recipe vegan. My goal and my hope for *Liquid Health* is to meet you right where *you* are on your path to better health, and to support *your* healthy lifestyle!

 "The best and most beautiful things in the world cannot be seen or even touched. They must be felt with the heart."
— HELEN KELLER

1 The *Liquid Health* Kitchen

*L*iquid Health is my eighth book, believe it or not (ironic, considering I never had the wish to write a book). Now that we've been on this journey together for more than 25 years, the equipment that I use for *Liquid Health* is more like friends or sidekicks than appliances. I know by now what works and what doesn't, and the equipment I use is reliable, dependable, and easy to use. I love that the companies who manufacture my *Liquid Health* tools have since partnered with me, in addition to supporting their customers and standing by their equipment. The following is a list of some of my absolute favorites:

TRIBEST'S GREENSTAR ELITE JUICER

Tribest's Greenstar Elite Juicer is my all-time favorite juicer. I start each day juicing wheatgrass with the Greenstar Elite. I like the fact that all the juice comes out of the machine in one pass; no need to keep running the pulp back through the machine. In fact, continuously running pulp through a juicer can heat up the pulp, defeating the purpose of raw food. I can run all types of fruits and vegetables through the Greenstar Elite—hard vegetables (carrots and beets), celery, and leafy greens like kale and spinach—some juicers only do one or the other. The Greenstar Elite is the most versatile juicer in the market, with a complete mastication system that provides you quality and quantity unsurpassed by other juicers on the market.

CITRISTAR

I love Tribest Citristar for juicing lemons, limes, and oranges. I do have a manual juicer, which is great for a quick job. But when a recipe needs a lot of juice, my Citristar couldn't be more valuable. What can I say, I'm a gadget girl. Plus, I prefer that it does the labor, instead of me.

TRIBEST'S SLOWSTAR JUICER

Tribest's Slowstar Juicer is a relatively new juicer on the market. It runs at a low 47 RPM, and it's great for juicing soft fruits and vegetables, like tomatoes and peaches. It can also mince. This is a must-have for making fermented foods (like sauerkraut).

DYNABLEND® (HIGH-POWERED HOME BLENDER)

Dynablend® is made by Tribest and has a 1.1 horsepower motor. It does everything other super-powered blenders do, for half the price. This blender just recently came on the market, and one of its most attractive features is that it has a glass pitcher. The glass pitcher won't dull with years of use (and is easy to clean). It also comes with a stainless steel utility scoop that acts as a tamper (and is also a one tablespoon measurement utensil). The Dynablend® has a variable speed dial from low to high, as well as three automatic settings. Tribest stands behind the Dynablend® with a 10-year warranty.

TRIBEST'S PERSONAL BLENDER

Tribest makes a personal blender, great for packing in your suitcase when you don't want to take your larger units on vacation or a business trip. The Tribest Personal Blender is also handy to keep in your car when you want to whip up something quick during your daily travels. Years ago, my family spent their Christmas at a rental property in Florida, where the rental's blender couldn't even blend watermelon. My trusty Personal Blender to the rescue! And it even works great as a nut grinder. It is convenient in your home as well, whether you have a family or whether you're single, as it can make custom, portion-controlled smoothies or mixtures that are perfect to everyone's preference.

VITAMIX (HIGH-POWERED BLENDER)

The Vitamix has a 2.2 horsepower motor and has a 5 to 7 year warranty, although their products tend to last much longer than that. I bought my first Vitamix almost 20 years ago, and it is still going strong. Consumer Reports has rated it the #1 blender in its class for the last 17 years. The Vitamix comes with a cookbook, containing a wealth of recipes and pictures to show you how to use your machine (as well as an instructional DVD).

NUT MILK BAG

I have tried many nut milk bags through the years, and you can't imagine my happiness when I found my search was over. My favorite nut milk bag is made by Rawsome Creations. You can purchase this nut milk bag directly from Rawsome Creations (www.rawsomecreations.com), or through major online distributors like Amazon. These bags are handmade in Bali, Indonesia, with part of the proceeds going to help to support Ibu Robin at the Yayasan Bumi Sehat Birthing Center, and the Yayasan Widya Guna Orphanage. (You can also directly help support the birthing center and orphanage; remember, a few dollars goes a very long way.)

For the thrifty among you, you can also use paint strainers as makeshift nut milk bags (which can be purchased at your local hardware store).

TRIBEST SOYABELLA

With Soyabella (a soymilk maker from Tribest), you can make fresh milk from beans, rice, and nuts in your kitchen. Soyabella makes delicious drinks like fresh soy milk and rice milk in as little as 15 minutes. For raw vegans, Soyabella makes delicious raw nut milks like almond milk and cashew milk in seconds. It is also great for making delicious pureed soups and porridges. The Soyabella also has different program settings that let you control the temperature.

WATER SYSTEMS

There is a lot of talk currently about the value and benefit of water. Be it water shortages, companies and/or countries buying water rights, or how much water to consume each day, the solution is simple. In addition to quenching your thirst, water helps the body's metabolism, blood circulation, and elimination of waste, balances blood acid levels, and helps to cool down or heat up your body temperature. But just like anything else in your life, you have to take matters into your own hands (or faucet) and do your homework.

I have town water myself (as opposed to the beautiful, clean well water I had as a child). But today, farmland is turned into housing developments, and overcrowding and pollution have made water (in addition to land and air) a precious commodity. After oxygen, water is the most basic need for a human's life and vitality (60 to 70 percent of our bodies are made up of water!)

On a cellular level, water is responsible for getting nutrients into your cells. It's also the way we flush toxins and waste from our bodies. With water playing such a pivotal role in our bodies, it only makes sense to be just as careful about what you drink as what you eat. And modern town water is loaded with chemicals like chlorine and fluoride, none of which are good for your body.

So, assuming that we don't want to haul our own water, how can we make the water we *do* have better? Believe it or not, I personally have *three* water systems. Did I mention that I'm a gadget girl?

Regency Elite Water Ionizer and Alkalizer

I have this countertop unit installed on my kitchen sink, so that all the water I drink I run through its filtration process. It's a six-stage filtration which removes bacteria, chlorine, and particles (even particles as small as 0.1 micron) while leaving the essential minerals intact. It also results in higher oxygen levels, which will be most apparent during exercise and physical labor. And, as strange as it sounds, it actually makes the water *wetter*. It changes the molecular structure of the water through electrolysis, which makes it more hydrating and quicker to refresh.

The system even lets you add alkaline to your water. The ideal alkaline level for the average person is 7.4, reached by eating and/or drinking more greens. Raw food promotes an alkaline body, whereas meats, processed foods, and stress can cause an acidic body. Think of it as your body being in a tug of war, trying to stay balanced.

Minerals are some of the most important nutrients the body needs, and yet mineral deficiency is common. Ionized water helps make the minerals you need more available. In addition to the filtrated water, I also add trace minerals to my smoothie every morning. The water ionizer rearranges the healthy minerals native to tap water, attracting alkaline and acidic minerals to separate chambers. The result is alkaline water containing essential calcium, magnesium, potassium, and sodium minerals. It also has excess oxygen, (at greater than a 2:1 ratio). Minerals that are ionized are much easier for the body to absorb.

Tribest's Duet Water Revitalizer

The Tribest Duet works by using the natural spiral movement found in nature. It spins the water within a magnetic field while releasing tiny amounts of minerals from the basket at the base of the pitcher, which in turn restores the water to its living, liquid crystalline state (with high levels of oxygen and vital energy).

The water in your body is already in a crystalline structure; when you drink water that has been converted into a crystalline structure, the water is easier for your body to use. Even after I run my tap water through the Regency unit, I always make sure to run it through the Duet Water Revitalizer.

Dancing with Waters, an insightful book on the nature of water, provides an in-depth look at water's unique qualities. It also offers instructions for creating full-spectrum living water, as well as how to add energetic enhancements. Its author, M.J. Pangman, is a walking encyclopedia on water!

And if you want to learn even more about water, be sure to read Dr. Masaru Emoto's books, including *The Hidden Messages in Water*, *The True Power of Water*, and *The Secret Life of Water*. I just purchased Dr. Emoto's book *Water Chrystal Healing: Music and Images to Restore Your Well-Being*, which contains CDs of music to improve the crystalline structure of your water. Dr. Emoto's research has been shown to produce beautiful crystals, which themselves suggest healing and well-being.

Megahome Water Distiller

I also have a Megahome Water Distiller. The concept behind distilled water is to boil it into steam, cool it, and then collect the pure water from the vapor. The main advantage of distilled water is that it is 100 percent boiled, sterilized, clean, safe, and environmentally friendly. Distilled water is hands-down the cleanest water. It is less acidic and is devoid of minerals. If you add a level teaspoon of baking soda to a gallon of distilled water, it makes a highly alkaline mixture. You can add minerals back in, such as liquid trace minerals. If you don't have a trusted source of clean, safe, high-quality spring water, distilled is easily your best choice. It is also the preferred choice when detoxifying or fasting, especially when you aren't sure of (or don't have) quality spring water available.

Megahome thinks of their water distiller as an artificial kidney, one that can filter all the harmful residues in the water and protect the quality of your drinking water. It is 100 percent H2O.

Some recipes, such as kombucha (see page 161) call for distilled water.

Takeya Flash Chill Iced Tea Maker

When I started taking permaculture classes (with Melissa Miles through Permanent Future) and Homesteading Herbalism classes (with Sue Hess—Farm at Coventry), I learned that herbs are good for a lot more than just seasoning our food—they can also offer lots of health benefits in the form of herbal teas. There are medicinal herbs that can be used for healing, including many that we think of as weeds. An easy way to ingest herbal teas is either through hot tea (using a French press) or my new favorite gadget, the Takeya Flash Chill Iced Tea Maker. You can even buy a fruit infuser attachment, which can then be used with the teas or to infuse the water.

2 Healing Ingredients

Once you see for yourself the healing benefits of the ingredients used in this book, you'll know why this book is called *Liquid Health*. Before now, you might have eaten a carrot just because it tastes good, or dropped a piece of celery in your soup for the salty flavor. But you're about to see that these amazing ingredients are in fact powerful healing components, and that learning to properly include them in your diet can have amazing results.

MACA

Maca root is a root native to the high mountains of Peru. It is a natural hormone balancer, providing health benefits to both men and women, and is often recommended for fertility problems, sterility, and other sexual disorders. It's also a libido enhancer, and helps to alleviate menopausal symptoms and painful menstrual symptoms. It's also a great source of energy; in addition to supporting your hormonal balance, it also restores and rejuvenates your adrenal glands to boost your energy and endurance.

COCONUT OIL

Coconut oil consists of 90 percent raw saturated fat, and is a building block of every cell in the human body. It contains healthy, healing, medium-chain triglycerides (MCTs).

COCONUT WATER

Not only is coconut water sterile, it has the same electrolytic balance as human blood. In other words, drinking coconut water is a lot like giving yourself an IV. In fact, medics in the Pacific Theater of World War II would use coconut water as an emergency substitute for plasma during transfusions. I love drinking coconut water after a good work out!

RAW HONEY

When consumed unfiltered and 100 percent pure, honey is not only antibacterial—it's *full* of vitamins and minerals, and is great for an energy boost. One third of our total diet is dependent (directly or indirectly) on the honeybee and the dozens of plants it pollinates. As an ingredient, honey works to relieve irritation in your mouth and throat by forming a protective film, making it a great cough medicine. Honey can also be used in wound care: its antibacterial, antifungal, and antioxidant properties make it great for treating wounds.

Interestingly, if you use local honey it will likely contain pollen spores picked up by the bees from local plants, which in turn will introduce a small amount of local allergens into your system. This can activate your immune system and, over time, will build up your natural immunities.

Many health care products today use honey because it attracts and retains moisture. The National Honey Board has a few you can try out for yourself:

Honey Hair Conditioner: Mix ½ cup honey with ¼ cup olive oil. Work a small amount through your hair until coated. Cover your hair with a shower cap and let sit for 30 minutes. Shampoo regularly and rinse.

Honey Body Moisturizer: Mix 5 tablespoons honey, 2 tablespoons rose oil, and 2 cups almond oil in a medium-sized bottle. Apply as needed onto wet skin.

Honey Almond Scrub: Mix 3 teaspoons honey, 1 teaspoon olive oil, and 6½ tablespoons of finely crushed almonds. Rub the exfoliating scrub on to your face gently and rinse with warm water.

The Organic Consumers Association published this Honey Lemon Cough Syrup recipe. Lemon helps to promote health by quickly alkalizing your body, while honey will kill most bacteria while soothing your throat.

To make, place a pint of raw honey in a pan on the stove on very low heat. Do not boil honey, as this will changes its medicinal properties.

Take a whole lemon and boil in some water in a separate pan for 2 to 3 minutes to both soften the lemon and kill any bacteria that may be on the lemon skin. Let the lemon cool enough to handle, then cut it into slices and add it to the pint of honey on the stove. Let the mixture cook over warm heat for about an hour. Then, strain the lemon from the honey, making sure all lemon seeds are removed. Let cool, then bottle in a jar with a lid and store in the refrigerator.

This syrup will keep for two months in the refrigerator. To soothe a cough, take ½ teaspoon for a 25-pound child, and 1 teaspoon for a 50-pound child (about 4 times as day or as often as needed). Adults can take 1 tablespoon doses.

TURMERIC

This spice is popular as a healing root in Indonesia. It is a blood purifier and is beneficial for many different health conditions, ranging from cancer to Alzheimer's disease, hepatitis, and more. It equalizes blood sugar levels and is useful for easing stomach cramps and indigestion. Health studies have shown that turmeric can be three times more effective at easing pain than aspirin.

WATERMELON

Watermelons are a natural diuretic and are great kidney and bladder cleansers. Rich in vitamin A and potassium, the melon also has a toning effect on digestion.

STRAWBERRIES

Strawberries are a mild diuretic and a natural painkiller—perfect for flushing out aches and pains from overexertion.

CELERY

Celery helps to curb one's cravings for sweets, and due to its high concentration of alkaline minerals (especially sodium) celery works to calm the nervous system.

BEETS

Beets are full of alkaline minerals like potassium and calcium, and are a great blood and liver cleanser. They help to build up the red corpuscles in the blood, and are full of beta-carotene, calcium, fiber, folate, iron, potassium, protein, and Vitamins B6, C, and K. They are good for healing cancer, cardiovascular disease, dementia, high blood pressure, and constipation, and are healthy for one's eyes and nerves.

APPLES

Apples help to regulate digestion and elimination (thanks to the natural digestive enzyme pepsin, which apples contain) as well as reducing cholesterol and enhancing mineral absorption. They are also a bowel regulator. Remember to store your apples in a cool location. (Now we know where the saying, "An apple a day keeps the doctor away" came from!)

ORANGES

Oranges are high in vitamin C and calcium. Don't forget to eat the white part of the meat closest to the skin—it contains the bioflavonoids which enhance the body's absorption of Vitamin C.

CABBAGE

Eating cabbage can be helpful with digestion. Cabbage has a high fiber content which helps to stimulate the digestive system while relieving constipation. Cabbage contains several cancer-fighting compounds, including lupeol, sinigrin, dilindolylmethane (DIM) indole-3-carbinaol (I3C) and sulforaphane, which may help to trigger enzyme defenses while inhibiting tumor growth. Cabbage is also one of the best natural remedies for stomach ulcers. A study at Stanford University School of Medicine found that fresh cabbage juice is very effective in treating peptic ulcers, due to its high glutamine content. This glutamine content is also believed to help those who are suffering from any type of inflammation.

Cabbage is also high in beta-carotene, which is great for your eyes, and its high vitamin C content strengthens the immune system. The lactic acid contained in cabbage helps to relieve muscle soreness.

PEAR

The quiet and unassuming pear is chock-full of vitamins A, B1, B2, C, folic acid, and niacin. They are also rich in many minerals, supplying the body with phosphorous, potassium, chlorine, iron, magnesium, sodium, sulfur, and a little calcium. But go easy on pear juice, as it does act as a diuretic and laxative.

CUCUMBER

Cucumbers are full of potassium and are valuable in balancing pressure (as well as helping gum and teeth afflictions). They are also great for fighting nail splitting, hair loss, and weight loss.

CARROTS

Carrots are full of magnesium and calcium, which help to strengthen your bones and teeth. Carrots contain Vitamins B, C, D, E, G, and K, and are rich in beta-carotene, a natural solvent for ulcers and cancerous conditions.

WHEATGRASS

On top of being a blood cleanser, wheatgrass also provides our daily requirement of chlorophyll, on top of more than 50 minerals and vitamins. Wheatgrass juice protects the lungs and blood from some of the air and water pollution.

SPINACH

Thanks to its high fiber and water content, spinach is a great liver cleanser, as well a great aid in preventing constipation and promoting a healthy digestive tract. Spinach is full of vitamin K, which is great for bone health, as it acts as a modifier of bone matrix proteins, while improving calcium absorption and reducing the urinary excretion of calcium. Spinach also contains an antioxidant known as alpha-lipoic acid which lowers glucose levels, and increases insulin sensitivity.

The risks for developing asthma are lower in people who consume high amounts of certain nutrients. One of these nutrients is beta-carotene, of which spinach is an excellent source. (Apricots, broccoli, cantaloupe, pumpkin, and carrots are also rich sources of beta-carotene.)

Now you know why Popeye loved his spinach!

PINEAPPLE

Pineapples contain bromelain, which is an active enzyme that serves as an effective anti-inflammatory agent.

LEMON

Lemons are amazing. Lemons (as well as limes, though to a lesser degree) are great for alkalizing the body. Lemons also neutralize the body, and possess antiseptic properties. Many people start the day by mixing lemon juice and water together and drinking it; it has great digestive properties and can ease heartburn, bloating, and other digestive issues.

Did you know that if you drink a glass of lemon water every morning it will actually kick-start your metabolism earlier? If you want to lose weight, start your day off by drinking lemon water. Also, if you drink hot lemon water it can offer relief from cold and flu symptoms while providing Vitamin C. Lemon juice is also an all-natural skin cleanser.

Lemons are also full of calcium, magnesium, and potassium.

CORN

Corn contains ferulic acid, which is an anti-carcinogenic compound. It also contains fiber, potassium, and thiamine, as well as lutein (an antioxidant).

DATES

Dates contain calcium, fiber, iron, magnesium, manganese, niacin, polyphenols (anticancer compounds), as well as potassium and Vitamin B6. Who knew that the humble date could be so packed full of nutrients?

BANANAS

Bananas contain fiber, potassium, tryptophan, Vitamin B6, and Vitamin C. They are good for relieving stress, anxiety, depression, high blood pressure, blood sugar swings, muscles, even teething pain, and sleeplessness.

AVOCADO

Full of fiber, folate, magnesium, monounsaturated fat, potassium, steroids (cholesterol lowering compounds, Vitamin B6, and Vitamin E, avocados are also noted as being good for your hair, high cholesterol, cardiovascular disease, cancer, blood sugar swings, and for alleviating insulin resistance.

BEAN SPROUTS

The first question people ask me when they find out I'm a vegetarian is, "Where do you get your protein?" Well, here's your answer, folks: sprouts are full of protein! Not only that, but bean sprouts are full of calcium, fiber, iron, protein, and sulforaphane (an anti-cancer compound) and Vitamin C.

PURCHASING ORGANIC PRODUCE

People always ask me: "Isn't purchasing organic produce expensive?" I've never seen a problem with treating myself—I'm worth it, after all—but I still try to buy smart. For example: I buy blueberries and strawberries by the case (preferably when on sale) and freeze them, so that I get not only the sale price, but the bulk price as well.

You can also save money by going directly to the food distributors (if your area allows for that). These are the same food distributors that the markets and restaurants buy from, and by going directly, you eliminate the middle men and their markups.

CSA (Community Supported Agriculture) is another great way to buy fresh produce locally and economically. You don't have to grow it, you get the chance to support local agriculture, *and* it's fresh.

Finally, you often have the option to grow it yourself. I have half an acre to myself in a small town, which has a fenced-in, raised bed garden. This year I grew strawberries, kale, spinach, peas, beans, carrots, beets, an assortment of tomatoes, melons, zucchini, eggplant, and, for the first time ever, asparagus. I also have blueberry bushes. In addition, not only do I grow culinary herbs, I also started growing medicinal herbs after I took my permaculture class (at Permanent Future) and herbalism classes (at Farm at Coventry).

You can also grow indoors, no matter what size abode you live in. You can sprout in jars or bags. Grow herbs in pots on your window sill. Grow tomatoes or greens on grow racks under grow lights. Just start growing!

3 Cleansing

A cleanse is basically spring cleaning for your body—getting rid of the gunk that accumulates over time and builds up in your body, slowing you down and making you feel worse. Since beginning to actively work towards a more dynamic lifestyle for myself, I have done numerous cleanses, following the same format each time—regardless of whether the cleanse was for one day or more than a week.

My basic process is this: I would juice apples to make apple juice, which I then combined with water. I would drink this—and only this—every 1½ hours, drinking 8 ounces each time (supported by supplements provided by my colon therapist). In addition, each day I would get a colonic that would help to clean out everything I was letting go—essentially, giving my body a rinse. Because your body doesn't need to work nearly as hard on a healthy raw diet (compared to the regular food found in a Standard American Diet) it has time to properly cleanse your body and get rid of the toxins that get stored in its tissues. Combined with the daily colonics, your body can clean out multiple layers of built-up waste attached to the colon wall.

Please note that getting a colonic every day is not mandatory when doing a cleanse or when fasting. A colonic is something that *I* chose to include in my cleanse regimen, but I realize that not everyone is comfortable with colonics, or they may not have them available in their locale. The main benefit of adding a colonic to a cleanse is that it speeds up the cleansing process by directly removing the toxins as your body is shedding them. But as with all things concerning your health, you need to do what you are comfortable with.

I try to start a cleanse on a Friday after work; that way, I can take things real easy over the weekend. Of course, in a perfect world I wouldn't have to do a cleanse *and* work at the same time—but I don't live in that perfect world, and I'm betting you don't either. During the work-week portion of a cleanse, I still stick to a juice-only diet, but I skip my usual workout routine—I feel that my body is already working extra hard cleansing itself. At night, I juice all of my apples for the next day, increasing my yield by adding water. I fill up all of my Ball® jars for the next day, and then pack them in the cooler when I go to work. At night (after work and after I finish preparing my juices for the next day) I take my shower, settle down, and go to bed early. It's important to try to give your body extra time to rest during the cleanse process—it does you no good to over-exhaust yourself.

On the last day of the cleanse (whenever that may be, whether 3 days or 10 days), I juice equal parts beets and kale, and drink that combo (still supported with supplements). I still have a colonic, which again helps to flush out any toxins that have been released from the body.

Here are a few recipes that I've found to be extremely helpful—and delicious—when going through a cleanse:

Cleanse Fast Drink

Prep: 10 minutes

   4 Granny Smith apples
   4 ounces water

Juice apples and combine with water. Store the juice in glass jars with lids, and shake it up when ready to drink to combine the apple and water.

Liver Cleanse Drink

Prep: 10 minutes

   Red beets
   Kale
   Water (optional)

Juice equal parts kale and red beets, combine, and drink.

During my cleanses, I like to work with a colon therapist. It's comforting to be seeing a medical professional every day of the cleanse—that way, they can check in on how you're doing, both emotionally and physically. If you don't have a medical professional you feel comfortable with, note that many raw restaurants have juices already juiced for you—you can check in with them. There are also also holistic health care professionals who can work with you, so that you don't have to go it alone. Alternatively, you could buddy up with a friend and cleanse together!

When my colon therapist and I discussed my doing a cleanse, she warned me that during the cleanse, I would be operating on another level—emotionally, physically, and spiritually. And it's true; one of the first things I learned is that the amount of food we eat—even in a healthy lifestyle—isn't necessary. We as a society eat for any number of reasons, many of them emotional and social, regardless of whether or not we're actually hungry. We eat because we're bored; we eat because it's "that time of the day;" we eat because we're celebrating; we eat because we're sad. What I find fascinating is just how little we really need to eat in order to sustain life. A cleanse allows you to really start listening to your body's needs, eating only when you are truly hungry. (Please keep in mind that, if you are diabetic, you *must* still eat regularly, no matter whether your stomach is growling or not.) And of course, as with any lifestyle or diet change, check in with your doctor before making any changes.

Besides losing weight (and realizing that you don't need to eat nearly as much food as you think) undergoing a cleanse will actually change the way your taste buds work—you will no longer even *want* to eat the Standard American Diet. Several years ago, when I held my Raw Challenge at Kimberton Whole Foods, I challenged the participants to exclusively juice, drink, and/or blend their meals for the first week. I wanted them to see for themselves how *good* a cleanse can make you feel, and the effect it can have on your tastes and preferences. They came back changed; they had lost weight, they were sleeping better, they no longer wanted to eat junk food, and there was an underlying glow of health to their skin. They felt *better*, emotionally and physically. (For those of you who wish to participate in your own "raw challenge," take a look at one of my previous books—*Raw Challenge*—which details my Raw Challenge Workshops on topics ranging from how to hold your own raw challenge to the mindset behind the workshops, the information presented, and the benefits involved. The book is full of attendee testimonials talking about personal growth and successes achieved through the Raw Challenge. It also has plenty of recipes for breakfast, lunch, and dinner—not to mention the items needed to set up your own healthy kitchen.)

Strangely, some people (myself included) report experiencing a caffeine high after their first cleanse (despite my not having had so much as a diet cola in 15 years). According to my colon therapist, it doesn't matter how long it's been; things like caffeine (and certain drugs, like LSD and codeine) stay in your cells for *years*. And not just substances—old emotions like anger and fear stay in your cells, too. And during my first cleanse, I *did* feel like my emotions were going up and down. By doing the cleanse and keeping up with the colonics, it got all of those leftover hormones and emotions out of my body. And when I had my second cleanse, I stayed calm—no caffeine high, no roller coaster of emotions.

With each cleanse you go through, you'll likely find yourself being even more careful about what you put in your body. After all, if you're going to go through the hard work of cleansing your body, why screw it up by putting junk food back in?

I know that there are hundreds of books out there on cleansing, with dozens of recipes to their name. But I tend to live a more simplistic life. Yes, I've tried tons of different recipes; but recently I've gotten to a place in life where I trust my judgment and know what works best for my body. And for my body, simple is best. If apple juice is what works best for me, then that's what I go with. It's already challenging enough to work, *and* cleanse, *and* make your own juices—let's not complicate it further by concocting a juice with 25 ingredients. You'll be annoyed trying to find all of the ingredients, not to mention preparing them all. Bottom line is, your body works better on a more simplistic level. I know gourmet dishes look beautiful, even *taste* beautiful, but they are also harder for your body to digest. There's no need to create a gourmet juice for fasting. "Keep it simple, stupid;" the K.I.S.S. Method remains as true now as it did back when, and works well not only in life, but when cleansing.

If I had to say what I think is the most important part of cleansing, it's to be gentle—to you and to your body. I didn't used to listen to my body; I would be sick and still trying to bulldoze through, thinking I had to be a super woman. That may be what the corporate world expects of you, but it's not fair for you to expect that of your body. The most important thing is for you to take care of yourself, while listening to your body. I find that my body is far smarter than my head when it comes to taking care of itself; it's a good indicator of what works and what doesn't work—and I'm not limiting that just to cleanses. I recently had someone request that I speak and demo at an event, very last minute. I said I couldn't; I was already booked for the month and just didn't have the time or the money. But though they kept pushing, my body let me know that no matter how much they asked, and no matter how good an opportunity it might be, it wasn't going to happen. Your emotions are a protection device. They let you know when something, be it a food or a human being, isn't working for you. And my body just plain felt overwhelmed. I listened to my body and said, "*No.*" And I immediately felt better; once you do your first cleanse and get rid of the toxins in your body, you'll find that it's much easier for you to connect with your body and to listen to it. Your body won't be numb or shut down any more!

4 Healing Stories

LISA MONTGOMERY

Over 25 years ago, I changed my diet because of food allergies (gluten, dairy, and peanuts) and candida. At the time, it seemed easier to list what I couldn't eat, as opposed to what I could. I felt overwhelmed, but after I got over my woe-is-me moment, I started to embrace what I could eat under my new diet plan—especially when I started to see health benefits *immediately*. Some of the health challenges that I had thought a result of me getting older turned out to have been the result of the food allergies and candida. The side effects I'd experience after eating those foods included sore throat, exhaustion, cloudy eyes, grogginess . . . the list goes on. My hands would even at times swell up, because my body was sending fluids to try and flush toxins out of my body. Thanks to the candida, I could go from diarrhea to constipation. But much to my delight, when I started to change my diet, my immune system strengthened (meaning I was no longer affected by non-food-based allergies, like bee stings or airborne allergens), while my vitality and well-being continued to return, stronger than ever.

After cleaning out my cupboards of everything I couldn't have, I tried every-thing. I went microbiotic for a while, then vegetarian. Finally, I settled into the raw food lifestyle, and have been predominantly raw for a good 15 years. This wasn't a planned journey, though; it just happened. Like in life, one stepping stone led to another. But as I made these changes, I felt healthier and healthier, to the point of euphoria. I no longer had sore throats, stuffy sinuses, groggy head, or clouded eyes. Where I had once been hyperactive, my energy level had become peaceful. I no longer felt like a pinball in a pinball machine. And my healthy diet not only changed how I felt physically, but how I felt emotionally and spiritually. Raw foods, for me, resonate down to my soul.

I was so passionate about the transformational changes I'd been experiencing that I started taking healthy cooking classes everywhere. I started with macrobiotic classes, and then switched to raw food classes. I became certified as a Health Care Coach at the Institute for Integrative Nutrition in Manhattan by taking classes on weekends. My healthy studies then took me to California, where I became certified as an Associate Raw Chef Instructor at the Living Light Culinary Institute of Raw Foods in Fort Bragg. I then went and took classes at the Natural Gourmet Institute in Manhattan, followed by lessons with Quintessence's certified Chef Mastery Program. To this day, I continue to take local classes as well; I am an avid learner, and I never want to stop learning and growing.

When I came back from my studies at the Living Light Culinary Institute of Raw Foods, I felt led to start monthly raw potlucks. I felt that people needed a support system so that they knew they weren't alone in living a healthy lifestyle. I started asking friends, who in turn asked their friends, and lo and behold, my first raw potluck had 65 people. Everyone who came had a blast, even if they were new to the whole "healthy living" thing.

For the next couple of years, as I continued to promote the raw food lifestyle to everyone who would listen, I had folks from all walks of life (including the press) saying that I should write a book. I kept telling them that I wasn't an author (I'm just a regular person, who wants to hear what I have to say?) until a friend finally said to me, "Would you just write the stupid book? Nothing is going to move forward until you write that dang book."

So, I took some time during Memorial Day weekend back in 2009 and started to write my first book: *Raw Inspiration: Living Dynamically with Raw Food*. Now, eight books later, I guess people *do* want to hear what I have to say—or at least what a regular person living a healthy lifestyle in corporate America has to say. I still do my day job as a sales representative for a packaging company, but it no longer controls me. It's just what I do for a living; it pays my bills. Know that you need to take control of your life. You and you alone are responsible for you.

If you had told me 25 years ago, when I first changed my diet, that these amazing happenings were around the corner, I would have said you were crazy. Once I changed my diet, my life's purpose became to promote healthy living, and all because of the personal experience I've had with how changing your diet can transform your life. I have more energy, but it's a peaceful energy. I have peace of mind and peace of heart. Even my heart used to be hyper. Now I have and feel peace, joy, and love in my heart.

Once I stopped eating the standard America diet, removing the cooked foods and meats that numb you to the point that you can't feel your emotions or what's going on in your body, I was able to connect with my emotions and repair the damage done throughout my life. If you aren't in touch with your emotions, you leave yourself vulnerable to hurt and heartache. Once you heal your body and heal your emotions, you have an opportunity to grow spiritually. I've been a person of faith for as long as I can remember, but it's only as a result of a healthy body and emotions that my spiritual life has been able to grow. With a quiet mind and a peaceful heart, God has had an opportunity to speak, and I've had the opportunity to hear. One of the biggest gifts we can receive is the divine guidance that we are all given. Now, having learned to trust myself and God, I'm able to actually listen.

You might be thinking to yourself, "Wow! If I start drinking wheatgrass, vegetable/fruit juices, and smoothies, am I going to have a powerful life transformation like you?"

My answer is emphatically *yes*. By now, you know that I want to live my life dynamically, and that liquid health is a key ingredient to my personal recipe for living a healthy life. Even though this transformation has been one with a lot of blood, sweat, tears, and work, it has all been well worth it. I can say that, from my own personal story, I wish all the blessings possible for your own personal transformation. You won't regret it.

Now run off to the kitchen and go make a green drink. Don't forget to toast to yourself, and to the first day of the rest of your life. Take it from me—I always want my tomorrow to be my best day ever!

JUSTINE BACON (PHILADELPHIA, PA)

"Be truthful, gentle and fearless."
—MAHATMA GANDHI

"Gratitude—it's what's for dinner!"
—JUSTINE BACON

Justine is a warm and playful Vinyasa teacher and inspirational writer. She teaches both heated and non-heated classes, as well as Pranayama at various locations in Center City Philadelphia and surrounding suburbs. In 2013, Justine co-founded Philly Yoga Factory, Philly's first all-donation-based yoga collective and serves as the organization's director and one of their teachers. She is the Center City Community liaison for Philly Area Yoga as well as a Pro-Ambassador for Jade Yoga.

A former Vitamix Demonstrator with a background in raw food and juicing, Justine creatively concocts healthy treats that taste like sinful favorites! Her favorite part? Sharing them with her family (and not telling them what's in it!). Music is in her soul, the ocean is in her heart, and the people closest to her are everything. In her free time, she loves stand-up paddle boarding whenever possible and outdoor cycling.

From Justine:

Just like anything worthwhile, it takes some time and effort to achieve a rhythm, a groove, a flow with what you're striving for. It might require a fall or two, and pieces of who you are now will break away in the process, but this isn't a bad thing. When we shed these pieces, we create the space for the greater parts of ourselves to fill in, take root, and thrive.

I have always loved food, from the time that I was able to eat it. My mother made my baby food from scratch, so I never used to think of my food—I just ate it. I was never one to question where it came from, who made it, what was in it, how it was raised, harvested, or what it was doing for me. My relationship with food was fairly black and white; healthy is healthy, unhealthy is unhealthy, food is good, and it's expected that you'll eat seconds on holidays.

As time went on, I learned more about food, the food industry and food culture. I became a label reader (and a messy business that can be, not to mention time consuming). This provoked a shift in my thoughts on food, and food became all about me—how can *this* food make me feel better, look better, and *be* better?

I spent July of 2011 in Guatemala, volunteering with the Whole Planet Foundation. While that is a story all its own, I can tell you that my relationship with food shifted to one word: *gratitude*. The most humbling moment of my life so far came while building a carbon-efficient stove for a family that cooked their food on an open fire on their dirt floor. We didn't speak the same language, so our communication was based on gestures, feelings, and just being together. I spent two days working on their stove. When they ate, I ate. Lunch for them one day was crackers and bottled cola. Lunch for me that day was crackers and bottled cola. Though they had nothing, they shared all they had with a smile and gratitude, and I could *taste* that. Judgment of food, judgment of myself, and what I ate broke off of me that day.

Holding our ideals in our hearts as we move toward our goals—food and otherwise—is all that we can ask of ourselves. Approaching any meal, ideal or not, with gratitude for it "just being," and for those who provide it to you, will lend gratitude for you "just being" as well. One thing is for sure—gratitude is a way of choosing food that is always practical, available, and affordable.

BARB (CLACKAMAS, OR)

Before I met her Barb was a mother of four very heavy-set kids—as a matter of fact, the entire family was heavy-set. She decided one day she was going to make a change in her family's life. She headed for the pantry, then the fridge, and then onto the snack cabinets, and completely emptied them out. Along with that decision came the strength to plunk down $500 for her very own Vitamix. She'd been hearing about these great machines from several different sources; however, like most people, she thought it was just a very expensive blender—that is, until she realized just how much of an impact it could really have on her and her family. That very same day she finally bought a Vitamix (along with all the necessary raw fruits and vegetables needed to jump-start her new lifestyle). In just four short months she completely changed the health of her entire family and healed her children of the diseases they were suffering from. Barb and her husband no long suffered from cholesterol problems, and she was able to rid all four of her children of the type 2 diabetes that had developed as a result of their obesity. As a result of Barb's strength and determination, she was able to help her family lose all their excess weight and become healthy again.

REMINGTON (SUNNYVALE, CA)

By the time Remington learned that he had cancer, the disease had already developed into stage 4. Cancer cells in stage 4 can spread to other lymph nodes, and even into the bloodstream, and travel throughout the entire body. In response, Remington decided to change his entire way of living and go completely natural— no radiation, no cancer treatment, nothing. Just a full-on natural eating lifestyle, using his Vitamix to cure himself of cancer!

LEIGH ANN (SUNNYVALE, CA)

A few years back, Leigh Ann was diagnosed with colon cancer. Unfortunately, by the time the cancer was discovered it had already spread extensively. Knowing that something needed to be done to slow the progression, Leigh Ann ran out to purchase a Vitamix and began using it religiously. Though it did not save her life, the use of her Vitamix allowed her to drastically slow the cancer's spread, prolonging her life and giving her as high a quality of life as possible for her remaining time.

JULIA (SUNNYVALE, CA)

Julia comes from an Asian family, and when I met her in a Costco, she was there specifically to purchase a Vitamix machine for a family member who had just been diagnosed with a tumor. Their doctor had strongly suggested that they run out to purchase a Vitamix as a tool for drastically changing their daily lifestyle and eating habits. The doctor strongly felt that, with an immediate changeover to whole food juicing, they could exponentially improve the patient's health. I spent the next several demonstrations working with the Julia, teaching her how to properly use her Vitamix machine while giving her the confidence and comfort to immediately start their new whole food juicing diet.

CINDY (SUNNYVALE, CA)

About 15 years ago, Cindy had her annual checkup with her doctor—a checkup which included a rectal exam, where some abnormalities were found. Upon further investigation (through a colonoscopy) it was determined that Cindy had developed some tumors in her colon, which needed to be promptly removed. During the surgery, Cindy's doctor was able to remove two of the larger tumors; however, there were several other tumors that were too small in size for surgical removal at that time. The solution suggested to Cindy was to simply wait for the tumors to grow to the size that they could be surgically removed.

   Not satisfied with this solution, Cindy took it upon herself to seek out a more effective solution. She discovered that the best solution was to get a Vitamix and start a whole food juice diet. Several months after her procedure, at one of Cindy's follow-up appointments, her doctor was astonished at the results. Through her diligent efforts, Cindy was able to not only stop the further development of the existing tumors, but she was able to completely rid her body of them. All of this turned Cindy and her doctor into believers of the healing powers of eating properly—but more specifically, whole food juicing using a Vitamix.

DANA MICHELLE STYER (CLACKAMAS, OR)

Dana Michelle Styer is a Vitamix representative and has touched the lives of many people as a result of her teaching and her demo-ing Vitamix products. The following are some of the healing stories from some of her clients as a result of blending, juicing, and changing their diet and lifestyle:

VALENTINA

August 2014, in a Costco in Sunnyvale, California. As the crowd dispersed while I finished a demonstration of the infamous Vitamix Tortilla Soup, a woman in her mid-50s approached my booth. She proudly announced to me that she's had her Vitamix for three years now, and shared this story of how it had completely changed her life.

Three years ago, Valentina knew she needed to make some drastic and immediate lifestyle changes. After much research and discussion with her doctor, she bought her first Vitamix machine and began a journey to better health and wellness. She did a complete 180 in regards to her health and dietary habits. She changed everything—her meals went from whatever she could grab to two Vitamix smoothies per day, one for breakfast and one for lunch, while dinner became an adequately proportioned sensible meal.

Through her habitual consistency, she has lost 140 pounds to date (and count-ing), and she's no longer pre-diabetic! Not only does she look great, but her skin is spectacular, almost to the point of glowing! Beaming with pride and joy of her accomplishments thus far, she knows that she still has more weight to lose; what excites her most is that she's making great life changes the "right way" by choosing to use her Vitamix on a daily basis for her healthy green smoothies!

FAYTHE

January 2014, in a Costco in Sunnyvale, California. All the green ice cream has quickly disappeared, along with an impressed crowd. Off to my right, I notice a woman discreetly watching my demonstration. After a brief pause as she worked up her courage, she makes her way over to my booth. Apparently, she'd decided to take the plunge and finally purchase a Vitamix of her own after seeing a demon-stration I'd presented in fall of 2013. She'd been searching for ways to make drastic life changes in both her life and the lives of her family; she'd tried every possible diet out there, to no avail.

Faythe shared with me how she had lost 40 pounds to date (even during the holidays), while her family, who would normally not even touch fruits and veggies with a tenfoot pole, are not only asking for smoothies on a daily basis, but are mak-ing the smoothies and ice cream themselves! Though it was an important decision to actually follow through with her purchase of a Vitamix machine, she's grateful she did; it's completely and utterly changed the lives of the people that are most important to her.

⑤ Recipes

UNDERSTANDING THE DIETS IN *LIQUID HEALTH*

With so many eating requirements involved in the more extensive diet plans—whether due to a medical reason (such as food allergies) or personal preference—it helps to know whether a given recipe is allowed. For this reason, I have marked each of the recipes in the following pages, for your convenience. Below is an overview of each diet type identified throughout the recipes.

Raw

Raw recipes are generally comprised of fruits, vegetables, nuts, and seeds. More importantly, raw recipes are not heated above 118°F. Heating above 118°F kills all the nutritional, enzymatic value of the food. As a result, your body receives the full nutrition benefits of the food. It is also easier to digest. You will have more energy, sleep better, and will feel healthier and happier.

Note that not all raw foodists are vegetarians; the myth of all raw foodists subsisting on nothing but carrot sticks is a common misconception. Some eat raw meat, cheese, and milk. The recipes in this book are all meat and dairy free, but if a person's diet is 80 percent raw, they are still considered to be a raw foodist. Raw foodists will also blossom natural wilderness rice, quinoa, buckwheat, chickpeas, and lentils to supplement their diets.

Gluten-Free

A gluten-free diet is just as it sounds—a diet that excludes all gluten, a substance found in wheat, barley, oats, and rye. A protein composite, gluten causes health problems, particularly in those allergic to it. Symptoms of gluten allergies include exhaustion after eating foods containing gluten, sore throat, runny eyes, and nose. It can also produce cranky or irritable moods. The strength of these allergies can vary, and some folks (those who suffer from full-blown celiac disease) can die as a result of eating wheat.

Paleolithic Diet, "Paleo" Diet

The Paleolithic Diet (or Paleo Diet, as it's more commonly called) is modeled after the so-called "caveman diet." Designed to emulate a Stone Age or hunter-gatherer diet, the Paleo diet recommends that people eat only the types of plants and animals consumed during the Paleolithic era, while avoiding foods such as dairy, grains, legumes, processed oils, and refined sugar (which were *not* available during the Paleolithic era).

The Paleolithic era lasted approximately 2.5 million years, and ended about 10,000 years ago with the arrival of agriculture and the domestication of animals. Prior to that enhancement in humans' ability to provide for themselves, their nutritional needs were based on what was available. Proponents of this diet feel that modern humans remain best suited to that selection—foods available prior to cultivation. They feel that the human metabolism is unable to adapt fast enough to handle many of the foods that have become available since the arrival of agriculture and beyond. In addition to restricting grains, legumes, and dairy products, humans should also be avoiding high-calorie, processed foods. And let's get real for a moment: *no one* should be eating high-calorie processed foods, regardless of which diet they follow.

Critics of the Paleo diet feel that there is sufficient evidence to indicate that humans did eat grains and legumes during that era; therefore, the diet can be approached with some degree of flexibility. Humans are much more nutritionally flexible than we might think, after all.

Regardless, meat, seafood, and other animal products still represent the staple foods of today's Paleo diet eaters (19–35 percent). The Paleo dieter consumes fewer carbohydrates, and limits themselves to non-starchy vegetables. Non-starchy fresh fruits and vegetables provide 35–45 percent of the Paleo daily calorie requirement, and are the Paleo dieter's main source of carbohydrates. For comparison, the typical standard American diet gets a lot of its carbohydrates from dairy products and grains (which are excluded in the Paleo diet). High fiber intake is still a part of the Paleo diet, but comes from non-starchy vegetables and fruit as opposed to grains.

The following food groups were either rarely or never consumed by *Homo sapiens* during the Paleolithic era; therefore, they are *excluded* from the Paleo diet:

- Dairy products
- Grains (wheat, rye and barley)
- Legumes (beans and peanuts)
- Processed oils

- Refined sugar
- Salt
- Alcohol or coffee

Veganism

Veganism entered into public awareness in 1944, when Donald Watson co-founded the Vegan Society in England. At that time, the diet referred to a non-dairy vegetarian lifestyle, later clarified as, "the doctrine that man should live without exploiting animals." Veganism's popularity has exploded since the turn of the millennium. Modern practicing vegans abstain from the use of animal products, in both their diet and their environment. Strict vegetarians—which are separate and distinct from vegans—do not consume animal products, although some vegetarians will consume eggs, dairy products, raw honey, and other animal-products, so long as no animal was harmed or killed in its production.

The degree to which a person is vegan or vegetarian is a matter of choice, and keeps in mind what works for their body, their environment, their planet, and their soul.

Juices and Elixirs

For optimum health results, one must first realize the importance of eating local, fresh, raw, and whole foods. Drawing on these proven sources of reliable ingredients, juicing and blending remain one of the easiest ways for your body to absorb all the nutrients you are digesting.

Remember how, when you were little and you didn't feel well, your mother might give you the infamous chicken noodle soup? The thought process here is the same, save that my version of chicken noodle soup has become consuming blended drinks and soups of fruits and vegetables, which have the advantage of being much easier for a body to digest, be it sick or healthy. Even when you are sick to the point that the simple act of eating becomes an effort, drinking blended drinks or juices lets you relax while the liquid magic does the rest for you.

"Peace is akin to an elixir to your soul. Once obtained, it brings you infinite inner strength for the trials you face. Grace during difficult times and expansive joy during the times of blessings. Recognize how you can feed your soul and in turn you create opportunities for your soul to feed you."

—WISDOM FROM THE TREE OF LIFE

V3

Prep: 5 minutes

> **3 medium to large tomatoes**
> **¾ cup green pepper**
> **1 stalk celery**
> **Sea salt, to taste**

Run the ingredients through a Tribest Juicer. Stir and drink.

Note: If you want to spice up this recipe, you could add a pinch of cayenne pepper or Tabasco sauce (note that this is not raw or fresh).

Melon Morning

Prep: 5 minutes

> **3 cups watermelon fruit**
> **1 piece watermelon rind**

Run the watermelon meat and rind through a Tribest juicer and drink. You can also add watermelon meat to your high-speed blender. Blend until thoroughly blended and drink.

NOTE FROM LISA

I love drinking watermelon juice after I get done exercising. It quenches my thirst, and if you want something to eat with just a little sweetness, drinking a little watermelon juice will curb your sweet tooth.

Lisa's Every Day Green Drink

Prep: 7 minutes

½ to 1 lemon, cut to fit juicer
1 cucumber, cut into spears to fit juicer
4 celery stalks
6 apples, cut into wedges to fit juicer
Handful of your favorite greens

Feed all ingredients into a Tribest Greenstar Elite Juicer. Stir and drink.

Note: You can adjust the above ingredients to taste, or even toss in some additional vegetables such as carrots, ginger, parsley, cabbage, or beets—whatever you have on hand will be fine.

Tomato Watermelon Juice

Prep: 5 minutes

2 cups watermelon fruit
2 medium-to-large tomatoes

Chop up all ingredients and run through a Tribest juicer. Alternatively, you can blend all the ingredients together in your high-speed blender.

The tomato in this recipe adds a little salty spice to the watermelon's sweetness, so that they balance each other out.

Banana Juice

Prep: 5 minutes

>   3 frozen peeled bananas
>   2 cups almond milk (see page 115)
>   6 Medjool dates, pitted
>   Raw honey and alcohol-free vanilla, to taste (optional)

Combine bananas, almond milk, and dates in a high-speed blender until smooth. You may wish to add raw honey or vanilla to kick it up a notch.

Apple Pear Juice

Prep: 5 minutes

>   3 apples cut to fit juicer
>   3 pears cut to fit juicer

Run apples and pears through a Tribest Green Elite Juicer. Stir and drink.
    Please note that you can juice the seeds, core, and stems—remember, nothing should be wasted!

Leftover Juice

R **V** **GF** **P**

Cucumber	Onion
Celery	Mint
Apples	Tomatoes
Greens	

When making a salad, I will occasionally run the leftovers through my Greenstar Elite Juicer to create a healthy, tasty recycled drink.

NOTE FROM LISA

Unfortunately I can't give the exact measurements for this drink. The point is to use whatever you have on hand, and run it through your juicer to create a new drink that doesn't waste anything. Or, you can take the leftover scraps and combine them with nuts to turn them into a nut pâté—using either the blank blade in your juicer, or else your high-speed blender. You can also take the scraps and combine them with flaxseeds, flavoring them and turning them into crackers to be dehydrated in your Tribest Sedona Dehydrator. I love how nothing is wasted in this lifestyle!

Pomegranate Orange Juice

R **V** **GF**

Prep: 5 minutes

4 oranges, peeled
½ cup fresh pomegranate seeds

Run oranges and pomegranate seeds through a Tribest Fruitstar or Slowstar Juicer. Stir and drink.

Watermelon Juice (Blender Method)

 **R V GF P**

Prep: 5 minutes

Watermelon meat, removed from rind

Cut watermelon meat from rind and blend together in a high-speed blender.

> ### NOTE FROM LISA
>
> By now, everyone knows I adore watermelon juice. I love to drink it after exercising. It quenches my thirst, it's cool and refreshing, and if you have a sweet tooth, a glass of watermelon juice will take care of the sweet cravings.
>
> It's also great for hydration, aids in weight loss, and serves as an anti-inflammatory and a diuretic, as well as being alkaline-forming.

Watermelon Juice (Juicer Method)

R V GF P

Prep: 5 minutes

Watermelon meat and rind, sliced

Feed watermelon meat and rind (cut in slices that will fit through the juicer's chute) and feed it into your Tribest Greenstar Elite Juicer. The Greenstar will juice the meat and the rind. The rind actually has more minerals and vitamins than the actual fruit.

Wheatgrass

Prep: 5 minutes

Wheatgrass

Run wheatgrass through your Tribest Greenstar Elite Juicer. Beginners should start by juicing 1 ounce per day.

> **NOTE FROM LISA**
>
> Wheatgrass is known for its healing and detoxifying properties. When you drink wheatgrass, it's best to sip the juice slowly and swish it around in your mouth for a while before swallowing. Wheatgrass has more than 50 minerals and vitamins— I call it liquid gold!

Wheatgrass & Lemon Juice

Prep: 5 minutes

2 ounces wheatgrass
Spritz of lemon juice

Run wheatgrass through your Tribest Greenstar Elite juicer. You can either run a wedge of lemon through the juicer or cut a lemon wedge and squeeze it by hand in to your wheatgrass. Stir and drink (by swishing).

> **NOTE FROM LISA**
>
> For some people, wheatgrass is a little too strong to be consumed straight. In the recipes above and on the next page, you will find a few options to try.

Wheatgrass/Apple

Prep: 5 minutes

> 8 ounces apple juice
> 2 ounces wheatgrass

Run apple juice and wheatgrass through your Greenstar Elite Juicer. Stir and drink (by swishing).

Wheatgrass Celebration

> 2 ounces wheatgrass
> 1 apple
> ½ cucumber
> Wedge of lemon

Run ingredients through your Greenstar Elite Juicer. Stir and drink (by swishing).

Pineapple/OJ

Prep: 10 minute

1 wedge pineapple
2 oranges

Either run fruit through your Tribest Greenstar Elite Juicer, or blend together through your high-speed blender.

Optional: Add tray of ice cubes and 1 banana for a very tropical drink. If you have a paper umbrella, set it on top of the glass with a straw—pamper yourself, and make yourself feel like you're basking in the island sun.

Pineapple-Apple OJ

Prep: 10 minutes

1 wedge pineapple
2 oranges
2 apples (remove core if blending)

Run fruit through your Tribest Greenstar Elite Juicer or blend together through your high-speed blender.

Pomaberry Slushee

Olivia de Maigret

Prep: 7–10 minutes **Yield:** 2 servings

1 cup fresh pomegranate juice
1 cup mixed berries (fresh or frozen)
1 tablespoon raw agave nectar
2 teaspoons fresh squeezed lemon juice
10 ice cubes
½ cup distilled water
2 sprigs fresh mint

Place all ingredients in a high-speed blender. Blend for about 1 minute, or until the mixture becomes smooth with the texture of a slush drink. Be careful not to over-blend, as the mixture will become too watery. Serve immediately in a tall clear glass. Garnish with mint leaves and enjoy!

What makes this recipe and its creator Olivia de Maigret so special is that she is only 12 years old! Olivia, her mom Kathryn and I had the pleasure of vacationing in Bali during October of 2014. We were there at the same time, staying in the same hotel, and even had the same tour guide. We all became instant friends, and we plan on staying connected forever.

Olivia created this recipe all by herself without anyone's help. I've heard people saying, "Oh, I can't eat healthy," or, "It's too hard," or, "I can't come up with recipes." But if Olivia can create this amazing recipe at the young age of 12, you too can eat healthy and create recipes—no matter what your age.

Note that if you are using store bought pomegranate juice, buy varieties that have no sugar added (Olivia prefers the POM brand).

PPAC

Prep: 10 minutes

> 2 peaches, remove pits
> 1 pear
> 1 apple (remove core if blending)
> 1 carrot

Run ingredients through your Tribest Greenstar Elite Juicer, or blend well in your high-speed blender.

Wheatgrass Delight

Prep: 10 minutes

> 2 ounces wheatgrass
> 1 apple
> 1–¼ slice pineapple
> 1 stalk celery
> ¼ cup spinach

Run ingredients through your Tribest Greenstar Elite Juicer. Stir and drink (by swishing). You can make this drink in your high-speed blender by eliminating the wheatgrass.

PPRC

Prep: 15 minutes

 ¼ slice pineapple
 ¼ cup fresh or frozen raspberries
 1 tablespoon pomegranates

Run ingredients through your Tribest Greenstar Elite Juicer. Stir and drink.

Berry Apple Juice

Prep: 7 minutes

 ¼ cup strawberries
 ¼ cup blueberries
 ¼ cup raspberries
 3 apples, cored

Slice apples to fit through the feeder of the juicer. Feed apples through the feeding tube of the juicer. Juice, stir and drink.

Strawberry Apple Juice

Prep: 7 minutes

¼ cup strawberries
2 apples, cored

Slice apples so that they can fit through the feeder of the juicer. Feed apples and strawberries through the feeder of the Tribest Greenstar Elite Juicer. Stir and drink.

Apple Carrot Juice

Prep: 8 minutes

2 apples, cored
6 carrots

Slice apples and carrots so they can be fed through the juicer. I do not peel the apples or carrots, as I prefer to use organic vegetables. Feed through juicer. Stir and drink.

NOTE FROM LISA

Carrots and apples help with digestion, as well as help minerals to be absorbed into your system. My Aunt Elsie used to juice carrot juice for my Uncle Joe daily when I was a little girl, and my Uncle Joe is still living today, well into his nineties.

How Do *You* Spell "Relief" Juice

Elysa Markowitz

Prep: 10 minutes   **Yield:** 2 servings

> 1 apple
> 6 carrots
> 2 slices purple cabbage

Cut apple, carrot, and cabbage into the appropriate sizes and alternate putting the different ingredients into the machine. Juice all ingredients.

Here's a tip: carrots are great for helping to push the produce through the juicing feeder.

Cabbage helps with digestion, and the pepsin in the apple is a digestive aid.

Fat Melt-Down Juice

Elysa Markowitz

Prep: 10 minutes   **Yield:** 2 servings

> 2 apples
> 2 pears
> 1 slice ginger

Cut apples and pears to fit into the machine. Juice all ingredients alternating with sliced apples, pears, and ginger. Stir and serve. Note that a little ginger goes a long way, so use ginger sparingly.

The high pectin content from the apple juice forms a gel in the intestines. This gel absorbs and dissolves toxins while stimulating the bowel, regulating elimination. Apples have Vitamins A, B1, B2, C, folic acid, and niacin, while pears are also rich in many minerals— supplying phosphorous, potassium, chlorine, iron, magnesium, sodium, sulfur, and a little calcium. Go easy on this juice because pear juices acts like a diuretic and has laxative effects.

Green Powered Juice

Elysa Markowitz
Prep: 10 minutes

4 handfuls wheatgrass	**4–6 carrots**
2 apples, cored	**1 thin slice fresh ginger**

Cut wheatgrass and feed it into the machine, alternating with sliced apples, carrots, and ginger. Juice all ingredients. Stir, serve and drink.

Wheatgrass is excellent for cleansing the blood. It provides us with our daily requirement of chlorophyll, while wheatgrass combined with apples and carrot juice offers the body Vitamin C, beta-carotene and a host of other vitamins to help cleanse and rebuild the blood. These ingredients help to cleanse the blood and strengthen the liver. Ginger is good for warming up the body on a cold day. The ingredients are great for your health, both individually and combined!

Falling into Winter

Elysa Markowitz
Prep: 10 minutes

4–6 carrots	**1 celery stalk**
1 kale leaf	**1 apple**

Prepare the ingredients to feed through the juicer. Feed through the juicer, stir, and serve.

Eating along with the seasons helps to keep our bodies in balance. These ingredients are typical fall or winter fare.

Carrot juice is one of the best balancers for our entire system. It is a rich source of pro-vitamin A and it contains vitamins B, C, D, E, G, and K. Rich in beta-carotene, it is a natural solvent for ulcerous and cancerous conditions. Taken in combination with kale, which is part of the cabbage family, the vitamin C content in the carrots is enhanced, making this drink particularly beneficial for ulcerous conditions and gum infections.

Green Green Juice

Elysa Markowitz
Prep: 10 minutes

1 kale leaf
2 celery stalks
2 apples
1 medium cucumber, unwaxed

2 romaine leaves
1–2 anise stalks (the white and
 the green stalk part)

Prepare ingredients to fit through the feeding portion of the juicer. Feed, stir and serve.

Chlorophyll is the best substance around for helping to balance our system. This juice is rich in chlorophyll from many sources—from the kale, romaine, and cucumber skins. The apple and anise help digestion, while celery calms the nerves and the cucumber is good for our hair and nails.

Orange You Glad It's Lemonade

Elysa Markowitz
Prep: 10 minutes

2 apples
2 oranges
¼ lemon

Prepare ingredients to run through the juicer. Juice and serve.

This is my new favorite lemonade. It combines three of my favorite fruits, it's cool, clean, and refreshing, and it's a great bowel regulator. Apples and oranges contain vitamins A, B1, B2, B6, and C, as well as folic acid and a host of minerals. This drink is a multivitamin for the day.

Menopause Tonic

Elysa Markowitz
Prep: 10 minutes

6 carrots

1 beet

6–8 spinach leaves

2 celery stalks

Prepare ingredients to fit through the juicer and feed into the machine. Juice all ingredients.

The carrots, beets, and spinach in this drink all work to cleanse the liver. The celery helps to calm the nerves, with its high concentration of sodium. Celery helps to reduce cravings for sweets. This recipe is good for energizing and balancing.

Because I was/am a vegetarian, I've never had problems with hot flashes—one of the major challenges for women going through menopause. Even if you haven't been a vegetarian for long, this juice will help support you through this process.

Blood Tonic

Elysa Markowitz
Prep: 10 minutes

1 cup wheatgrass

4–6 carrots

1 beet

½ cup Italian parsley

2 celery stalks

Prepare ingredients to feed through juicer; feed. Stir and drink.

Wheatgrass is one of the best blood cleansers. It is high in chlorophyll, which is a molecule that closely resembles the hemoglobin found in red blood cells. Parsley is also full of chlorophyll, and stimulates oxygen and metabolism, as well as cell respiration and regeneration. Parsley combined with the pro-vitamin-A–rich carrots, sodium-rich celery, and alkaline mineral-rich beets aid in building the red blood cell count. Who could ask for a better blood tonic?

Who knew that that sprig of parsley that restaurants put on your dinner plate all these years as a garnish was so good for you?

Pulsating Parsley Juice

R V GF

Elysa Markowitz
Prep: 10 minutes

6 carrots
1 beet

8 spinach leaves
¼ cup fresh parsley

Prepare ingredients for juicer. Feed through juicer, store, and serve.

This is a great blood cleanser juice that will help you rebuild your blood. Spinach juice contains a high concentration of alkaline minerals and is especially strengthening to the teeth and gums. Because of its high oxalic acid content it should be used moderately. Do not drink a lot of spinach juice, or else you may find yourself exercising all day to metabolize the oxalic acid.

Spinach also contains folic acid, potassium, magnesium, Vitamin, K, C, and lutein for healthy eyes.

Wheatgrass Cocktail

R V GF

Elysa Markowitz
Prep: 10 minutes   **Yield:** 2 servings

1 handful wheatgrass
8 carrots
1 lemon

Juice all ingredients except the lemon. Hand squeeze a lemon into each glass. Run the lemon wedge around the edge of the glass. Wheatgrass juice protects the lungs and blood from air and water pollution.

One of my favorite books written about wheatgrass is *The Wheatgrass Book* by Ann Wigmore. Ann Wigmore really brought wheatgrass, sprouts, and raw living food to the forefront. Many in the modern era have benefited from Ann, whether it be directly from her books or by learning from those who did.

Sweet Popeye Blend

Elysa Markowitz
Prep: 10 minutes

½ cup fresh spinach
½ cup arugula
8 carrots
2 slices fresh anise

Cut carrots and anise into pieces that fit and let feed into the machine. Juice all ingredients.

Spinach is said to be one of the most beneficial foods for the entire digestive tract, especially for the alimentary section (your stomach through to your small intestine) and the large intestine. Eaten raw, spinach is one of the most cleansing, reconstructive, and regenerative foods for the intestinal tract. It is also effective for helping the gums and teeth stay healthy. Arugula is stimulating for the liver and lungs. As with other dark green leafy members of the cabbage family, arugula is a rich source of calcium and is full of phytochemicals—recommended as a cancer preventative food by the American Cancer Society.

NOTE FROM LISA

When you read how power packed the vegetables and fruits in these recipes are, it should be obvious as to why we named this book *Liquid Health*. Reading these descriptions always confirms my decision to eat healthy. These recipes are just power packed for your health!

Yummy for the Tummy

Elysa Markowitz
Prep: 10 minutes

> **6 carrots**
> **1 apple**
> **2 celery stalks**
> **¼ cup fresh parsley**

Cut carrots and apples into pieces that fit and feed into the juicer. Juice all ingredients. Feed the parsley in stem first.

Parsley is high in iron and is another blood builder. Apples are high in Vitamin C, which helps prevent colds, flu, and intestinal infections. It helps the body's elaborate defense system fight against bacterial infections. Carrots build the blood and celery calms the nervous system.

Omega 3 Oil Blend

Elysa Markowitz
Prep: 10 minutes   **Soaking time:** 2–4 hours

> **4 oranges**
> **2 grapefruit**
> **½ cup fresh parsley or cilantro**
> **2 tablespoons flaxseeds soak 2–4 hours, no rinsing necessary**

Peel and cut the oranges and grapefruit into pieces so that they fit in to the machine and juice. In a blender, mix the soaked flaxseeds, parsley, or cilantro with the juice. Serve in a fancy glass, garnished with parsley or cilantro.

Flaxseeds have 24 percent omega-3 oils (as compared to fish, which has 2 percent). Flax is a mercury-free, toxin-free source of essential fatty acids.

Tangible Life Orange Drink

Elysa Markowitz
Prep: 10 minutes   **Soaking time:** 8–12 hours

4 tangerines
6 oranges
1 lime
2 tablespoons sunflower seeds (soaked 8–12 hours, rinsed)

Peel and cut the tangerines and oranges into pieces that fit into the machine and juice with half the lime, unpeeled. In a blender, mix the soaked sunflower seeds with the juice until smooth and creamy. Serve in a fancy glass and garnish with a lime wedge.

Rinsing the hulls off the sunflower seeds can be done by adding more water, floating them to the top, and pouring them away.

Sunflower seeds are rich in calcium, phosphorous, and iron, as well as vitamins A, D3, and several of the B-complex vitamins. Also, they contain a trace amount of fluorine which may account for the claim that they are good for teeth.

In the Pink with Zinc Drink

Elysa Markowitz
Prep: 10 minutes

4 apples
1–2 bananas
½ cup dried cranberries
2–4 tablespoons soaked pumpkin seeds (soaked 8–12 hours, rinsed)
1 lemon

Cut the apples into pieces that will fit into the machine and juice. In a blender, mix until smooth the soaked pumpkin seeds with the apple juice, bananas, and dried cranberries. Then, add lemon juice to taste. Serve in a pretty glass and garnish with lemon wedges.

Keep blending until the drink is thoroughly smooth. To make a thicker drink, add more bananas; to thin, add more apple juice or water.

Pumpkin seeds are high in zinc which is good for preventing prostrate problems and helps to strengthen our immune system. Cranberries help to keep bladders in balance, while lemons stimulate the lining of your stomach to make enzymes. Apples and bananas both contain a wide array of vitamins and minerals that support health.

Pro Bone O'Drink

Elysa Markowitz

Prep: 10 minutes   **Soaking time:** 8–10 hours

6 oranges
½ lime
2 tablespoons flaxseeds, soaked 2–4 hours, no rinsing necessary
3 tablespoons sunflower seeds, soaked 8–12 hours rinsed

Peel and cut the oranges into pieces that will fit into the machine and juice. In a blender, mix the soaked flaxseeds and sunflower seeds with the juice until smooth and creamy. Serve and garnish with orange wedges.

Blend with less juice at first until the mixture is creamy. Then, add the rest of the ingredients and thoroughly blend.

Sunflower seeds are rich in protein as well as calcium. There are six grams of protein in one tablespoon of sunflower seeds. This drink helps to build stronger bones.

Jae's Favorite

Jae Choi
Prep: 10 minutes

- **6 carrots**
- **2 apples**
- **2 celery stalks**

Cut the apples and carrots to fit into the juicer. Juice all ingredients.

All three of these ingredients are good for digestion. When food can be processed and eliminated with ease, it retains nutrients and expels toxins promoting better functioning of other body systems.

Sweet Apple Juice

Prep: 7 minutes

- **2 to 3 cups tomatoes**
- **1–½ slice pineapple**
- **1 squeeze of lemon juice**
- **1 teaspoon mint (spearmint or wintergreen)**
- **1 teaspoon raw honey**

Slice the tomatoes and pineapples to fit through the chute of your Tribest Slowstar Juicer. Run the tomatoes, pineapple, and mint through your juicer. Squeeze lemon to taste and stir in one teaspoon raw honey. Stir and drink.

Carrot Apple Ginger Juice

Prep: 7 minutes

> 1 cup carrots
> 1 cup apples
> 1 sliver ginger
> Ginger, to taste

Slice ingredients to fit through the feed section of the Tribest Elite Juicer. You do not need to remove the seeds, stem, or skin of the apple. All parts of the apple will be juiced. Feed the ingredients through the juicer. Stir and drink. Note that you can change the ingredient portions of this recipe, based upon whether you like more carrot then apple, or vice versa. Use what you have and use the ingredients you like.

Carrot Beet Celery Juice

Prep: 10 minutes

> 1 cup carrots
> 1 cup beets
> 1 large stalk celery

Cut the beets to fit in to the Tribest Greenstar Elite Juicer (no need to peel the beets). As you may have learned by now, in many cases the skin is the most nutritious part of the fruit and/or vegetable. Run the carrots, beets, and celery through the juicer. Stir, drink, enjoy, and feel energized. Feel free to switch up the proportions to your liking.

Carrot Beet Celery Juice Ginger

R **GF**

Prep: 10 minutes

> 1 cup carrots
> 1 cup beets
> 1 large stalk celery
> 1 sliver ginger

Prepare the ingredients such that they fit into the chute of the Tribest Greenstar Elite Juicer. Feed the ingredients into the juicer. Stir and drink.

I went to Bali in October 2014, and in addition to falling in love with the people and the land of Bali, I fell in love with their cuisine and spices. Ginger is used a great deal in Bali, and has so many healing benefits that I find myself slipping ginger into everything now.

Ginger is great for digestion, motion sickness, and—believe it or not—hangovers (to name a few).

Broccoli, Apple, Celery Juice

R **GF** **P**

Prep: 10 minutes

> 1 cup broccoli
> 1 cup apple
> 1 large stalk celery
> 1 tablespoon lemon juice
> 1 teaspoon raw honey

Slice ingredients to fit into the feeding tube of the juicer and run the broccoli, apple, and celery through the juicer. Squeeze lemon and stir in one teaspoon raw honey until well-blended. Drink and enjoy.

Pineapple, Apple, Mango, Mint, Beet, Honey Juice

Prep: 10 minutes

   1 (1-inch) slice pineapple
   1 large apple
   1 mango, pitted
   1 tablespoon mint
   1 large red beet
   1 teaspoon raw honey

Slice ingredients to fit through the feeding tube of the juicer. Run the pineapple, apple, mango, mint, and red beet through the juicer. Stir in the raw honey, then stir and drink.

Pineapple Apple Sunset Juice

Prep: 10 minutes

   1 (1-inch) slice pineapple
   2 large apples
   1 teaspoon mint
   ⅛ cup parsley
   ¼ cup greens (lettuce, spinach, kale . . . your choice)

Slice the ingredients to fit through the feeding tube of the Tribest Greenstar Elite Juicer. Run ingredients through the juicer and juice. Stir and drink.
   Feel free to add a squeeze of lemon juice and a touch of raw honey.

Broccoli/Strawberry/Pineapple Juice

Prep: 10 minutes

> 1 cup broccoli
> 1 cup organic strawberries
> 1 (1-inch) slice of pineapple
> 1 squeeze of lemon juice

Prepare the ingredients to feed through the feeding tube of the Tribest Greenstar Elite Juicer. Juice the broccoli, strawberries, and pineapple. Squeeze in a splash of lemon juice, stir the drink until blended, and drink.

As always, feel free to change the proportions to your tastes and availability of ingredients. Always, *always* buy organic strawberries. Strawberries are among the dirtiest foods to be grown non-organically. They are sprayed heavily with pesticides during conventional farming.

Apple-Celery-Broccoli Orange Juice

Prep: 10 minutes

> 1 cup (or 1 large) apple
> 1 large stalk celery
> 1 cup broccoli
> 1 orange (meat and juice)
> 1 teaspoon raw honey

Prepare the ingredients (except honey) to fit the tube of the juicer. Run the prepared ingredients through the Tribest Greenstar Elite Juicer. Stir in the raw honey. Stir until well-blended. Drink and enjoy.

Ginger Lemon Honey Juice

Prep: 10 minutes

1 sliver ginger
2 lemons (meat and juice)
1 teaspoon raw honey
Water, to taste

Slice the lemons to the size that they can fit through the feeding tube of your juicer. Juice the lemon and the skin. Add one sliver of ginger. Stir in a teaspoon of raw honey. Add water to taste.

If you want the juice to be tart, don't add too much water. If you want your lemon juice to be milder or sweeter, add more water and up the amount of lemon juice. If you want to kick the juice up a notch, add a dash of cayenne pepper.

Broccoli Celery Orange Juice

Prep: 10 minutes

1 cup broccoli
1 large stalk celery
2–3 oranges (meat and juice)
Water, if necessary

Prepare ingredients to fit through the tube of the juicer. Run the broccoli, celery and oranges through the juicer. You will be juicing the orange meat and skin. Stir to taste; add water if you wish the juice to not be as tangy. Leave as is if you want the juice to have more punch.

Pineapple Carrot Juice

Prep: 7 minutes

2 cups carrot
1–2 (1-inch) slices pineapple

Size the ingredients to fit through the feeding tube of your juicer. Feed the ingredients into your juicer. Stir and drink.

Pineapple Carrot Apple Celery Juice

Prep: 10 minutes

1 (1-inch) slice pineapple
1 cup carrots
1 cup apple
1 large stalk celery

Prepare ingredients to fit through the feeding tube of the juicer. Juice, stir, and drink.

Orange Cucumber Juice

Prep: 7 minutes

2–3 oranges (meat and rind)
1 large cucumber

Prepare ingredients to feed through the feeding tube. Juice, stir, and drink.

When you aren't sure how juicy or tasty your ingredients are, feel free to add another orange or less rind. Add another cucumber. Kick it up with a little lemon juice. Dilute with water.

Immune Juice

Prep: 10 minutes

1 cup (or 1 large) apple
1 large beet
2 oranges, juiced
1 cup carrots

Prepare ingredients to fit through the feeding tube. Juice, stir, and drink.

Apple Ginger Juice
aka Doctor's Orders Juice

Prep: 7 minutes

> 1 slice ginger
> 3 apples

Slice ingredients to fit through the feeding tube of the juicer. Juice, stir, and drink.

Apple Pie Drink

V **GF**

Janet Binger, Solle Specialist (www.onesolle.com/jbinger)
Prep: 7–10 minutes

> 10–12 ounces apple juice
> 1 package of CinnaMâte™ (from Solle Naturals)

Juice apples in your juicer. Stir in a package of CinnaMâte™ and mix well. Serve either cold with ice, or hot like hot apple pie. This product helps with sugar and alcohol cravings, and will improve sugar assimilation and improve stomach comfort. This product is all-natural and does not contain GMOs or any artificial sweeteners.

Strawberry-Mango Coulis

Prep: 15 minutes

> 3 cups strawberries, hulled
> 1 cup mango, cubed
> 1 cup dates, pitted and packed
> 1 tablespoon lemon juice
> ½ tablespoon lime juice
> Water (as needed)

Combine ingredients in a high speed-blender and use water as needed to blend well. Refrigerate in a glass jar with lid.

Watermelon-Strawberry Thirst Quencher

Prep: 15 minutes

> 3 cups watermelon
> 1 cup strawberries
> 1 lime, juiced
> 2 dates, pitted
> 1 tray ice cubes

Combine the above ingredients in a high-speed blender.

Smoothies

If I was ever forced to eat just one kind of meal for the rest of my life, I would choose smoothies in a heartbeat. I am a bona fide smoothie nut (or should that be a smoothie fruit?) and the reasons why are endless—they come in as many varieties as you can dream up: they're good for you; they're easy to make *and* easy to digest. You don't have to be a brain surgeon or a chemist to make a great smoothie; the smallest child can throw ingredients in a blender and push the button (with parents' supervision). Mom and Dad: on days when you're rushed and feeling overwhelmed—make a smoothie. Everyone will be glad you did. I hope these recipes inspire you to create your own smoothie concoctions!

I have several different bases that I use for making smoothies:

- Water
- Young Thai coconuts (water and meat)
- Nut milk
- Juice

Strawberry Orange Smoothie

Prep: 5 minutes

> 4–6 ounces fresh or frozen strawberries (with stems and leaves)
> 2 oranges (peeled and quartered)
> Handful of greens
> 3 bananas
> 1 tray of ice cubes
> Water (to cover ingredients)
> 1 tablespoon raw honey
> Sprig of fresh mint (optional)

Place all ingredients in a high-speed blender and blend until the mixture comes to a smooth consistency.

Green Apple Smoothie

Prep: 5 minutes

> 2 green apples, quartered and cored
> Handful of greens
> 3 bananas
> 1 tablespoon raw honey
> 1 tray of ice cubes
> 16 ounces water

Combine ingredients in a high-speed blender until smooth. Blend and drink.

Blueberry Grape Smoothie

Prep: 5 minutes

½ cup frozen or fresh grapes
½ cup frozen or fresh blueberries
3 bananas, peeled
1 young Thai coconut (meat and juice)
1 tray ice cubes
1 tablespoon raw honey

Combine ingredients together in a high-speed blender until smooth. If you don't have a high-speed blender, please use whatever blender you have available.

OPENING A YOUNG THAI COCONUT

It took me years to figure out the easy way to open a young Thai coconut. Now, I can open a young Thai coconut in seconds. First, place the young Thai coconut on a cutting board. In your other hand, hold a cleaver and start chopping with the back end of the knife, cutting a circle around the top. Pour the juice into blender, setting the opened coconut on the counter. Scoop out the meat with your ice cream scooper. Before I found the ice cream scooper method, I would scrape out the meat using spoons from my kitchen, but as the meat can sometimes be very tough and rubbery, the spoons would end up bent. Learn from my mistakes—use the ice cream scoop method, and don't ruin your spoons!

Peach Orange Smoothie

Prep: 7 minutes

2 oranges, peeled
2–3 bananas, peeled
3 peaches, pitted
1 tablespoon raw honey
⅓–½ cup water
1 tray ice cubes
Raw cacao nibs (optional)

Combine ingredients in a high-speed blender until smooth, hence the name smmooottthhhiiiee! Optionally, you can add raw cacao nibs sprinkles on top of the smoothie. Who said breakfast can't look good, taste good, feel good, *and* be good for you?

NOTE FROM LISA

Sometimes I'll use juice as the liquid part of my smoothie (mostly orange juice). The juices give the drink extra flavor, freshness, and lightness.

Chocolate-Peach-Orange Smoothie

Prep: 7 minutes

> 1–2 tablespoons raw cacao
> 2 oranges, peeled
> 2–3 bananas, peeled
> 3 peaches, pitted
> 1 tablespoon raw honey
> ⅓–½ cup water
> 1 tray ice cubes
> Raw cacao nibs (optional)

Combine ingredients in a high-speed blender until smooth and well blended. Optionally, you can add raw cacao nibs on top of the smoothie as sprinkles.

Berry Nice Smoothie

Prep: 7 minutes

> ½ cup raspberries
> ½ cup blueberries
> 1 tablespoon raw honey
> ½ cup strawberries
> 3 bananas, peeled
> 2–3 cups water
> 1 tray ice cubes

Combine ingredients in a high-speed blender until smooth. Pour and drink.

I love making this smoothie in season, especially, when you can get fresh berries.

Peach Strawberry Smoothie

Prep: 7 minutes

3 peaches
2 bananas
1 cup strawberries
2 cups fresh squeezed orange juice
1 tray ice cubes

Blend ingredients together in a high-speed blender until well blended.

Strawberry Peach Tomato Smoothie

Prep: 7 minutes

3 peaches
½ cup strawberries
1–2 cups tomatoes (this becomes your juice)
1 tray ice cubes
1 tablespoon raw honey

Blend ingredients together in a high-speed blender until well blended.

Demo Delight Smoothie

Prep: 7 minutes

1 cup fresh strawberries
1 orange, peeled
2–3 bananas
1 tablespoon raw honey
1–2 tablespoons raw cacao
1 tray ice
Water, add enough for desired smoothness

Blend ingredients together in your high-speed blender.

NOTE FROM LISA

I usually make this smoothie for demos, primarily because I like myth-busting. People can't believe that you can actually have chocolate-flavored food and have it still be good for you. Just remember: raw chocolate *is* considered a super food. Healthy food can taste good, be easy to make, and still be good for you. This smoothie is loved by people young and old.

Cinnamon-Fig-Banana Smoothie

Prep: 7 minutes

3 figs, stems removed
2 bananas, peeled
1 tablespoon raw honey
1 teaspoon cinnamon
1 tray ice cubes
⅓–½ container water
Raw cacao nibs (optional)

Blend all ingredients together in a high-speed blender until well blended and pour into glasses. Optionally, you can sprinkle the top of smoothie with raw cacao nibs. Note that this would be a raw recipe without Shilajit.

CINNAMON

Cinnamon increases the pancreas's ability to utilize insulin, which in turn benefits insulin resistance. Cinnamon also helps the body convert sugar into energy, and is great for weight management. It also helps to treat/prevent intestinal viruses, the flu, moving pain, rheumatism, and cold hands and feet. In the past, I'd always just used cinnamon for culinary purposes—but now you can see how it's fantastic for your health as well!

Dandelion Dreams

 GF

Prep: 7 minutes

> 3 dandelion leaves
> 2–3 bananas
> ⅛ to ¼ teaspoon Shilajit
> 1 tablespoon raw honey
> 1–2 cups spring water
> 1 tray ice cubes
> Raw cacao nibs, sprinkle on top of smoothie (optional)
> Wedge of pineapple (optional)

Blend ingredients together in a high-speed blender until smooth.

Dandelion is rich in vitamins A, C, D, and B complex, and in trace minerals such as magnesium. Dandelion is known to have the highest Vitamin A content of all greens. Dandelion is not only great to add to your smoothies and/or juices; you can incorporate it in your salads, spreads, breads, and jams. Because dandelion is a little bit bitter, I tend to add raw honey to help sweeten the taste of the smoothie. (This would be a raw recipe if you eliminated the Shilajit.)

HIMALAYAN SHILAJIT POWDER

Shilajit is a powder which is harvested by hand, and then dried at a low temperature. Containing over 85 minerals, Shilajit is said to remove weakness from the body and build strength as a result. I started taking Shilajit after my acupuncturist recommended it to me. You can purchase Shilajit from Natural Zing and Sunfood. I immediately went out and purchased a pouch and began using it in my smoothies every morning. A month later, when I went back to my acupuncturist, he told me that my pulses had never been better. Since that time I have consistently improved and continue to get stronger.

Peach OJ Smoothie

Prep: 10 minutes

    3 peaches, pitted
    2 oranges, peeled
    2–3 bananas, peeled
    1 tablespoon raw honey
    1 tray ice cubes
    ½ cup water
    Raw cacao nibs (optional)

Combine all ingredients together (except raw cacao nibs) in a high-speed blender until well blended. Pour smoothie into glasses. Optionally, sprinkle raw cacao nibs, a few to a handful, on top of the smoothie. Note that this recipe would be considered Paleo if you exclude the raw cacao nibs.

Pineapple Smoothie

Prep: 5 minutes

    1½ inch thick slice fresh pineapple
    3 bananas
    1 tablespoon raw honey
    1 tray of ice cubes
    12 ounces raw almond milk

Blend ingredients together in a high-speed blender until smooth.

Vanilla Crème Smoothie

 R **GF**

Prep: 7 minutes

> 2 tablespoons alcohol-free vanilla
> 1 tablespoon Singing Dog vanilla, alcohol free
> 9 dates, pitted
> 16 ounces raw almond milk
> 1 tray ice

Combine ingredients in a high-speed blender until desired consistency is reached. You can also add extra ingredients to help support your health and well-being, such as liquid aloe vera, Shilajit, or trace minerals. If a tray of ice is too chilling for you, try freezing your bananas and add water to equal the amount of one tray of ice.

Creamsicle Morning

 **R** **V** **GF**

Prep: 5 minutes

> 1–2 oranges, peeled
> 1–2 cups almond milk
> 2–3 bananas, peeled
> 1 tablespoon alcohol-free vanilla
> 1 tray ice cubes

Combine ingredients in a high-speed blender and serve.

Strawberry Chai Smoothie

Prep: 7 minutes

    2–3 bananas, peeled
    1 tray ice cubes
    1 cup frozen strawberries
    1 tablespoon raw honey
    Chai milk (enough to cover all ingredients)
    Handful of raw cacao nibs
    1–2 tablespoons raw cacao (optional)

Combine ingredients in a high-speed blender until blended.

Mango Madness Smoothie

Prep: 10 minutes

    2 cups mango chunks (frozen or fresh)
    2 cups peach chunks (frozen or fresh)
    1–½ cups freshly squeezed orange juice
    ¼ teaspoon almond extract
    ¼ teaspoon cinnamon
    2 bananas, peeled (optional)
    Almond milk (enough to cover all ingredients)

Combine ingredients in a high-speed blender until smooth. I also have made this recipe using fresh mango and peaches, and have added ice cubes for an additional chill to the smoothie (if desired).

Cool & Fresh Smoothie

Prep: 5 minutes

> 2–3 pears, cored
> 8 ounces coconut water
> 1 tray ice cubes
> 3 bananas, peeled
> 1 tablespoon raw honey

Combine ingredients in a high-speed blender until smooth.

Raspberry Cinnamon Morning Smoothie

Prep: 7 minutes

> 4 ounces organic raspberries (frozen or fresh)
> ½–1 tablespoon cinnamon
> 8 ounces almond milk
> 2–3 bananas, peeled
> 1 tablespoon raw honey
> 1 tray ice cubes

Combine ingredients in a high-speed blender until desired consistency is reached.

Neapolitan Smoothie

 GF

Prep: 7 minutes

> 8 ounces strawberries (with stems)
> 1–2 tablespoons raw cacao
> 1–2 tablespoons vanilla
> 12 ounces almond milk
> 2–3 bananas, peeled
> 1 tray ice cubes
> 1 tablespoon raw honey

Combine ingredients together in a high-speed blender.

Pumpkin Spice & Everything Nice Smoothie

 R **GF**

Prep: 7 minutes

> 3 bananas, peeled
> 4 ounces fruit, pumpkin, or butternut squash (peeled if pumpkin or squash)
> 1 tablespoon raw honey
> 1 tray ice cubes
> 8–12 ounces raw almond milk
> ½–1 teaspoon pumpkin spice or to taste

Combine ingredients in a high-speed blender and blend until desired consistency is reached. Pumpkin Spice typically includes cinnamon, ginger, clove, and nutmeg. If you don't have pumpkin spice at home, you can use these individual spices or come up with your own blend. Experiment; feel free to become a mad scientist in your kitchen!

"The Justine Machine"

 GF

Justine Bacon
Prep: 10 minutes

1 cup water
¼ cup raw almonds
1–3 teaspoons raw honey or raw agave
2 tablespoons cacao powder
1 tablespoon peanut butter (or 2 tablespoons peanut butter powder)
1 large (or 1½ small) frozen bananas, peeled

2 tablespoons frozen blueberries
4–5 baby carrots
1 large romaine leaf
A small pinch of spinach leaves
½ cup ice

Blend the above ingredients together in a high-speed blender for 30 seconds. Maca is a great add-on, though you can also substitute hemp seeds or walnuts for the almonds. You can jazz up your drink with a splash of vanilla and for a twist, sprinkle a dash of cinnamon.

Please note these measurements are to taste. I highly encourage you to adjust to your tastes and make it your own.

PPRC Smoothie

 R **V** **GF** **P**

Prep: 10 minutes

1 young Thai Coconut (juice and meat)
1 wide slice of pineapple
⅓ cup raspberry

1 orange, peeled
1 tablespoon pomegranate

Combine ingredients together in a high-speed blender until very smooth.

Parsley Peach Smoothie

Prep: 10 minutes

3 peaches
1 dash of Shilajit
3 bananas
2 dandelion leaves
Handful of parsley

1 tablespoon raw almonds, soaked
1 tray of ice cube
8 ounces water (optional)
1 tablespoon raw honey

Combine ingredients in a high-speed blender until smooth. Pour and serve.

Beyond The Works Smoothie

Prep: 10 minutes

2 tablespoons vegetarian protein powder
½ cup cabbage
2–3 leaves dandelion including stalk
⅛ teaspoon Shilajit
1 teaspoon maca powder
2 tablespoons raw cacao
8 ounces coconut water

1 tray ice cubes
1 small slice fresh turmeric
2 bananas
½–1 teaspoon cinnamon
¼ cup raw almonds
1 tablespoon raw honey
¼ cup blueberries

Combine all of the above ingredients in a high-powered blender. Blend and drink.
I feel like this smoothie gives you all the super power energy and healing a girl could ask for—or at least until I come up with another super-powered drink! Hope you enjoy it as much as I do.

The Works Cousin Smoothie

Prep: 7 minutes

3 bananas
2 dandelion leaves including stalk
⅛ cup green cabbage
1 sprig to 1 handful of fresh parsley
1 tablespoon raw honey
1 tray ice cubes
1 cup orange juice
¼ cup organic strawberries

Combine ingredients in your high-powered blender. Blend; pour in to your favorite pretty glass and drink.

Tropical Madness

Prep: 7 minutes

1 mango, pitted
1 papaya, pitted
1 banana, peeled

Combine ingredients in a high-powered blender until well blended. You can either peel the mango or papaya or leave the skin on. The high-powered blender will blend it up so that you won't have the skin texture in your mouth. Blend until well blended or desired consistency. If you wish the smoothie to be thinner, add water or a little orange juice.

Papaya Lime Smoothie

Prep: 7 minutes

    1 papaya, pitted
    1 banana, peeled
    1 teaspoon to 1 tablespoon lime juice
    1 cup ice cubes

Combine ingredients in a high-powered blender until smooth. Drink and enjoy!

Papaya Pineapple Smoothie

Prep: 5 minutes

    1 papaya, pitted
    1 (1-inch) slice pineapple

Blend ingredients together in a high-powered blender until smooth. Drink up.

Tropical Smoothie

 R **GF**

Prep: 7 minutes

> 1 papaya, pitted
> 1 (1-inch) slice pineapple
> 1 banana, peeled

Combine ingredients in a high-powered blender until smooth. This is a tropical, refreshing drink.

Orange Banana Smoothie

 **R** **V** **GF** **P**

Prep: 7 minutes

> 2 oranges, juiced (remove pulp)
> 1 banana, peeled

Combine ingredients in a high-powered blender until smooth. I think this smoothie combo was the very first smoothie I ever drank. I loved it then and I love it now. It's simple but it tastes good and is good for you.

Orange Banana Mango

Prep: 8 minutes

> 1 banana, peeled
> 1 mango, pitted
> 3 oranges juiced

Blend the ingredients together in a high-powered blender until desired thickness.

BAM Smoothie

Prep: 7 minutes

> 1 banana, peeled
> 1 avocado, meat
> 1 mango, pitted
> Water or juice, as needed

Blend ingredients together in a high-powered blender until smooth. If the smoothie is too thick add water and/or your favorite juice to your desired consistency.

Choc-Mint Smoothie

 R **GF**

Prep: 7 minutes

> 2 bananas, peeled
> 2 tablespoons raw cacao
> 1–2 tablespoons fresh mint to desired minty flavor
> 1 tray ice cubes
> Fresh spring water, enough to desired consistency

Combine ingredients in a high-powered blender until desired smoothness. Add water to create desired thickness.

Bunny Smoothie

 **R** **V** **GF** **P**

Prep: 10 minutes

> 1 handful lettuce
> 1 cup carrots
> 3 large apples juiced

Combine ingredients in a high-powered blender until smooth.

CCC Smoothie

Prep: 10 minutes

- 1–2 cups cashew milk
- 2 bananas, peeled
- 1–2 tablespoons raw cacao
- 1 tablespoon cashew butter
- 1 tablespoon raw honey

Blend ingredients together in a high-powered blender.

Date and Banana Smoothie

Prep: 10 minutes

- 1 cup cashew milk
- 1 banana, peeled
- 4 Medjool dates, pitted
- 1 teaspoon vanilla

Combine ingredients together in a high-powered blender until smooth. Drink up!

Chocolate Dreams

Prep: 5 minutes

> 1 cup chilled almond or cashew milk
> 1–2 tablespoons raw cacao
> 1 tablespoon raw honey

Blend ingredients together in a high-powered blender. I love chocolate, so you can bet I always go for the heavier amount of chocolate in any drink! But if you don't want the chocolate to be too strong, back off on the chocolate.

If you can't handle (or don't like) raw cacao, please feel free to substitute carob for raw cacao in any of the recipes.

Body Strengthener Smoothie

Prep: 7 minutes

> 2 bananas
> 1 cup almond milk
> 1 tray ice cubes
> 1 tablespoon tahini
> 1 tablespoon raw honey

Blend ingredients together in a high-powered blender until smooth. Drink and enjoy. Don't you feel stronger already?

Berry but Simple Smoothie

Prep: 5 minutes

> 1–2 cups almond or cashew milk
> 1 cup strawberries
> 1 tablespoon raw honey

Combine ingredients together in a high-powered blender.

NOTE FROM LISA

● ●

I always have a half gallon Ball® jar of nut milk on hand in my refrigerator. That way it's ready to go first thing in the morning, and when I'm making my breakfast smoothie all I have to do is pour the milk into the blender's pitcher (along with the other ingredients). Set yourself up for success, make it easy on yourself and have the nut milk ready to go when you need it!

Coconut Wonder Smoothie

Prep: 10 minutes

> Meat of 1 Thai coconut
> Juice of 2 Thai coconuts
> 3 Medjool dates, pitted
> 1 teaspoon vanilla
> 1 teaspoon spirulina

Blend ingredients together in a high-powered blender. Blend, serve, and drink.

Orange Cucumber Smoothie

Prep: 12 minutes

> 3–4 oranges, juiced
> 1 cucumber, juiced
> ⅛ cup parsley
> 1 teaspoon Spirulina

Blend the ingredients together in a high-powered blender.

Papaya Pineapple Smoothie

Prep: 7 minutes

> 1 papaya, pitted
> 1 (1-inch) pineapple slice
> 1 lime, juiced
> 1 cup coconut water

Blend together the ingredients in a high-powered blender until smooth.

Basic Green Smoothie

Prep: 7 minutes

2–3 bananas
Handful of greens
1 tray ice cubes
4 Medjool dates, pitted
1 cup spring water

Combine ingredients together in a high-powered blender.

Chaca Maca Smoothie

Prep: 7 minutes

1 cup almond or cashew milk
2 bananas
1–2 tablespoons raw cacao
1–3 teaspoons maca powder
1 tray ice cubes

Blend ingredients together in a high speed blender. Reduce the milk for a frostier, thicker smoothie. If you wish this smoothie to be frostier, don't blend as long.

Cucumber-Apple-Carrot Smoothie

Prep: 7–10 minutes

1 cucumber
2–3 apples
2 large carrots
1 banana
1 tray ice cubes

Blend the ingredients together in a high-powered blender. You can either juice the apples and carrots in advance, or combine with the banana and ice, or you can cut and core the apple and blend all ingredients together in a high-powered blender. You will have more fiber if blended. It's up to you to decide the texture you want. Keep in mind that your blender can blend vegetables—it's not limited to just fruits, nuts, ice, and superfoods.

Tropical Fruit Madness

Prep: 10 minutes

4 mangosteen (fruit only, no shell)
1 lizard fruit (fruit only)
2 bananas
2 tangerines, meat and juice
1 tray ice cubes

Blend ingredients together in a high-powered blender until smooth. The more exotic ingredients in this recipe can usually be found in multicultural and Asian markets, as well as some grocery stores.

Tropical Amazement Smoothie

Prep: 10 minutes

- 1 mango, pitted
- 1 papaya, pitted
- ¼ cup strawberries
- ¼ cup blueberries
- 1–2 tablespoons raw cacao
- 1–3 teaspoons maca
- 1 cup cashew milk
- 1 cup coconut milk
- 1 tray ice cubes
- 1 tablespoon raw honey

Blend ingredients together in a high-powered blender. Blend and drink!

Pineapple, Coconut Milk Smoothie

Prep: 5 minutes

- 1 (1-inch) pineapple slice
- 1 cup coconut milk
- 1 teaspoon mint

Blend ingredients together in a high-powered blender. Add ice cubes and blend to chill and thin the smoothie if desired.

Strawberry Pick Me Smoothie

Prep: 5 minutes

> 1 cup strawberries
> 1 cup almond milk
> 1 tablespoon raw honey
> 1 tray ice cubes

Blend ingredients together in a high-powered blender until smooth.

Lisa's SuperGreen Smoothie/Juice

Prep: 11 minutes

> 1 handful holy basil
> 1 handful parsley
> 1 handful kale
> Carrots
> Beets

Run ingredients through juicer and juice; alternatively, blend together in a high-powered blender. The carrots and beets provide the liquid for this drink; add as many as you like for desired drink amount.

Pineapple Coconut Banana Smoothie

Prep: 10 minutes

> 1 (1-inch) pineapple slice
> 1 young Thai Coconut (meat and liquid)
> 1 banana
> 1 tray ice cubes

Blend ingredients together in a high-powered blender until smooth. Drink and enjoy.

Mango Coconut Valencia Smoothie

Prep: 10 minutes

> 1 mango, pitted
> 1 young Thai Coconut (meat and liquid)
> 2 Valencia oranges, meat and juice
> 1 tray ice cube
> 1 tablespoon raw honey (optional)

Blend ingredients together in a high-powered blender.

Healing Smoothie

Warren Chambers, Elements Personal Care, Inc., Director of R & D
Prep: 10–15 minutes

1 stalk kale
1 cup organic strawberries (frozen or fresh)
½ cup peaches (frozen or fresh)
¼ cup beets (frozen or fresh)
1 cup of organic yogurt (with probiotic such as acidophilus and bifidus)
3 tablespoons raw clover honey (or any raw honey)
1 teaspoon cinnamon
2 cups ice

Blend ingredients together in a high-powered blender until well blended.

NOTE FROM LISA

Warren created this healing smoothie after two bouts with stomach cancer and having to deal with kidney failure (due to the increased doses of chemotherapy). His condition left him needing oral chemotherapy for the rest of his life. Warren wanted me to share with you how important he feels eating and drinking the proper foods and nutritional liquids, as well as exercise, are, and how it will improve your quality of life. Warren does not claim that this recipe will work for you—but it *does* work for him.

Peach Raspberry Smoothie

Jessica Javage

Prep: 5 minutes

1 cup sliced peaches
½ cup raspberries
¼ cup blueberries
¼ cup spinach
¾ cup unsweetened almond milk
3–4 ice cubes

Mix ingredients in blender until smooth. Enjoy!

Jessica Javage is a trainer for Fitness Trainers Incorporated, a personal training company located in Malvern, PA. During college she studied kinesiology and loved learning about the human body; she was especially fascinated by her nutrition courses. It was there she realized the importance of a careful and healthy diet in addition to exercise.

Jessica learned more about the raw diet when she began personal training for Lisa in July of 2014. After realizing how strong and healthy Lisa was, she began incorporating raw food practices into her own diet. Since then, she has seen overall strength improvements in her body (and is hooked on several of the smoothie recipes). Jessica is a firm believer that eating raw will positively impact your energy and happiness levels.

Green Smoothie

 **R** **V** **GF** **P**

Dana Michelle

4–5 Lacinato Kale Leaves
7–8 fresh or frozen strawberries
1 frozen banana
Small handful of raw almonds
¼ cup frozen three-berry blend (blueberries, blackberries, raspberries)
4 ice cubs
1 cup water

Place all ingredients into your high-speed blender and select variable speed 1 and increase to high. Blend on high for roughly 1 minute, until you reach a silky smooth consistency.

SMOOTHIE ESSENTIALS

These are just a few of the things I typically have on hand:

- Spinach
- Kale
- Carrots
- Pineapple
- Grapes (I prefer green grapes)
- Bananas

Milks

When people make the switch over to a healthy diet, one of the hardest foods for them to eliminate is milk. What will I put on cereal? What will I drink with my meal? Not to worry; this chapter shares some of my favorite milk recipes. In the Standard American Diet, most people limit their milk intake from cows, while the more adventuresome among them branch out to goat's milk. Regardless of what type of milk you're used to, you'll be able to find something to match your tastes among these healthy milk alternatives. Your options are virtually endless!

Basic Almond Milk

Prep: 10 minutes

> 2 cups raw soaked almonds
> 12 dates, pitted
> 1–2 tablespoons alcohol-free vanilla
> 6 cups water

Combine ingredients in a high-speed blender and blend on high speed until thoroughly blended. Place nut milk bag or strainer in a large bowl and pour milk through bag. Milk the milk bag until all the milk comes out. Store milk in a large sealed canning jar in your refrigerator. You can freeze the pulp and save for later to make crackers, croutons, or scones. Alternatively, you can save it and turn it into almond pulp pâtés. This would be considered a raw recipe without the vanilla.

Brenda's Almond Milk

R **V** **GF** **P**

Brenda Hinton, Rawsome Creations
Prep: 15 minutes   **Yield:** about 2½ cups

> 1 cup raw almonds (soaked 6–8 hours in cool water)
> 3 cups water

Rinse and drain the soaked almonds thoroughly. Place drained almonds in a high-speed blender along with enough water to cover the nuts. Blend until smooth, about one minute. Add remaining water and blend briefly. Strain blended mixture through "More Than a Nut Milk Bag" (www.rawsomecreations.com) and catch resulting milk in a bowl or pitcher.

Using two milk bags makes smoother milks and creams. You can use one, but adding a second one nestled inside the first in your pitcher creates an extra filter for catching smaller grains and yielding a very fine cream for desserts.

Hemp Milk

V **GF**

Prep: 10 minutes

> 1 cup hemp seeds, soaked
> 5 dates, pitted
> 1 tablespoon alcohol-free vanilla
> 3 cups water

Combine ingredients in a high-speed blender. Place nut milk bag in a large bowl and pour the blended mixture through the nut milk bag. Milk the nut milk bag. This liquid now becomes your milk. Store the milk in a large canning jar with lid in your refrigerator. The pulp can be saved to make other raw dishes.

Raw Sesame Power Drink

Dawn Light
Prep: 15 minutes

> 1 cup sesame seeds
> 3–4 cups filtered water
> Raw honey or raw coconut crystals, to taste
> 1 teaspoon maca powder
> 1 teaspoon mesquite powder
> 1 tablespoon chia or Salba® seeds per serving

Grind sesame seeds in a blender or coffee grinder. Grind until seeds are milled, but not congealed (if using a coffee grinder, put the ground sesame seeds into a blender).

Add 3–4 cups water and sesame seeds to the blender and blend for 30 seconds. Strain through a fine mesh "nut milk" bag (I like to use a nut milk bag with a drawstring). Close the drawstring and set it in a strainer that is on top of a deep bowl (which it fits onto perfectly), and then let it strain out of the bag until it is almost done. Then squeeze the rest of the nut milk out of the sesame pulp.

Return the sesame milk to the blender with remaining ingredients (except chia or Salba® seeds). Blend until mixed well. Pour into glasses, add 1 tablespoon chia or Salba® seeds, and stir well. Continue to stir the seeds around so they do not congeal at the bottom of your glass. After 15 minutes, the seeds are considered sprouted, and you have a yummy power drink. Store unused drink in the refrigerator.

Banana Lasse

Raw Chef Dan

Yogurt Blend
1 young Thai coconut (½ cup meat, chopped)
¼ cup water
1½ teaspoon lemon juice
1 teaspoon agave
¼ teaspoon sea salt
3 drops Live Live™ propolis

Lasse
1 cup ice, crushed
½ ripe banana
¼ teaspoon cardamom

Combine both together and enjoy.

Almond Milk

Tribest
Prep: 15 minutes   **Soak:** almonds, 6–8 hours

1 cup almonds, soaked and drained
2 cups water
1 tablespoon maple syrup
1 teaspoon vanilla

Blend the above ingredients together until smooth and creamy. Strain liquid in a milk bag or fine strainer using a large bowl. Store in a sealed glass jar. Serve cold in glass.

Maple Almond Milk

Tribest
Prep: 25 minutes   **Soak:** almonds, 4–6 hours

1 cup almonds, soaked/rinsed (2.5 ounces)
0.8 liter or approximately 3 cups (27 fluid ounces) filtered water (fill to the lower line in Soyabella chamber)
2–5 tablespoons maple syrup (grade B is best)
1 teaspoon alcohol-free vanilla
1–2 pinches sea salt

Fill the chamber with 0.8 liter (approximately 3 cups or 27 fluid ounces) of filtered water (to the lower line).

Fill the milk screen with soaked almonds and attach to the heat unit, turning counter-clockwise. Make sure it is secure.

Follow instructions for making raw nut milk.

Pour the unflavored almond milk in a glass container. Combine almond milk with maple syrup, vanilla, and sea salt.

Chill before serving.

Chocolate Cashew Milk

Raw Chef Dan

Prep: 15 minutes

3½ cups water
½ cup cashews
¼ cup cacao powder or nibs
1 tablespoon coconut butter
2 tablespoons agave
1 teaspoon vanilla
½ teaspoon sea salt

Blend all the ingredients together in a high-speed blender. Chill and serve.

For a smoother drink, you can strain the milk through a nut bag, which removes the nut pulp. You can also save the nut pulp and turn it into crackers, croutons, scones, or nut flours. Also, try serving it to your pets or wildlife in your backyard.

Elaina's Nut Nog

Elaina Love
Prep: 20 minutes   **Soak:** almonds, 8–24 hours

1 cup almonds, soaked
¼ cup pine nuts
2½ cups filtered water
2–3 frozen bananas, cut into chunks
4–5 medium dates, pitted (soak if firm and use the soaking water in place of water)
½ teaspoon nutmeg
½ teaspoon ground cloves
1 teaspoon vanilla extract
2 teaspoons flax oil
Pinch Celtic sea salt

Blend the nuts and water, and strain the pulp out using a nut milk bag.

Combine the milk mixture with the remaining ingredients in a high-speed blender and blend until smooth.

Nut Nog

Joel Odhner
Prep: 15 minutes

2 cups almond milk
4 dates, pitted
½ banana (frozen works best)
½ teaspoon vanilla
Pinch cardamom
Nutmeg to taste

Combine the above ingredients together in a high-speed blender. Store in a glass jar. Chill and serve.

Egg Nog

Janice Innella
Prep: 20 minutes

> 3 cups almond milk or Brazil nut milk (you make Brazil nut milk the same way that you make almond milk)
> 2 cups cashews
> 2 young coconuts (meat only)
> 2 vanilla beans
> 1 teaspoon nutmeg
> Pinch cloves
> ½ teaspoon garam masala
> 3 teaspoons stevia or ½ cup agave or 6 tablespoons raw honey
> 1 teaspoon cinnamon (or to taste)

Blend together well in a high-speed blender until creamy. Chill for a few hours. Serve with a sprinkle of nutmeg on top for garnish.

Un-Egg Nog

Prep: 15 minutes

> 2 cups almond milk
> 3 fresh bananas
> ¼ teaspoon Sun Organics alcohol-free vanilla extract
> ¼ teaspoon cinnamon
> Pinch sea salt
> 2–3 dates pitted
> ¼ teaspoon nutmeg, grated (or to taste)

Place all the ingredients in a high-speed blender and blend until smooth. Add additional dates if you wish the nog to be sweeter. Serve immediately with a dash of grated nutmeg on top.

Live Almond Nog for Holiday Comfort

Victoria Boutenko

Serves: 4   **Prep:** 15 minutes   **Soak:** almonds, overnight

1 cup raw almonds, soaked overnight
2 cups water
4–5 dates, pitted
1 teaspoon nutmeg, ground
¼ teaspoon sea salt (optional)

Thoroughly blend ingredients together in a high-speed blender until smooth. Strain mixture through a nut milk bag. Pour into a jar and chill.

Strawberry Coconut Milk

Prep: 5 minutes

6 ounces strawberries, fresh or frozen
1 young Thai coconut (meat and liquid)
1 tablespoon vanilla
1 tablespoon raw honey
3 bananas
1 tray ice cubes

Combine ingredients together in a high-speed blender until smooth.

Cashew or Brazil Nut Milk

 V **GF**

Prep: 5 minutes

> 2 cups raw cashews or 2 cups Brazil nuts
> 1 tablespoon alcohol-free vanilla
> 12 Medjool dates, pitted
> 6 cups water

Combine ingredients in high-speed blender until thoroughly blended. Place nut bag over a large bowl. Pour mixture through nut bag and milk the bag. The liquid that comes out through the nut bag will now become your milk. Store milk in the refrigerator in a ½ gallon canning jar with lid. You can also save the pulp and turn it into crackers, croutons, or scones.

Almond and Cashew Milk

 V **GF**

Soak: Raw almonds, 8 hours or overnight   **Prep:** 5 minutes

> 1 cup raw soaked raw almonds
> 1 cup raw cashews
> 1 tablespoon alcohol-free vanilla
> 12 Medjool dates, pitted
> 6 cups water

Combine ingredients in high-speed blender until thoroughly blended. Place nut bag over a large bowl. Pour mixture through nut bag and milk the bag. The liquid that comes out through the nut bag will now become your milk. Store milk in the refrigerator in a ½ gallon canning jar with lid. You can also save the pulp and turn it into crackers, croutons, or scones.

Almond Milk Smoothie

Kimberton Whole Foods

Soak: Almonds, 8 hours or overnight
Prep: Almond milk, 10–15 minutes; Smoothie, 7 minutes

Almond Milk
2 cups, raw almonds, strained
2–3 cups spring water
Vanilla, non-alcoholic; I use 2 teaspoons
    or more as I love vanilla
12 Medjool dates, pitted
6 cups water, pure

Smoothie
1 tray ice cubes
3 bananas, peeled
4–6 ounces blueberries
Almond milk, enough to cover all of the
    above in your blender
1 tablespoon raw honey
Raw cacao powder, to taste

Almond Milk

Let almonds soak overnight in water (for better digestion). In the morning rinse and drain the almonds. Then put them in your blender or jar. Add 2–3 cups of clean (spring) water along with the vanilla, dates, and a pinch of salt. Blend well. Pour the almond milk in the nut bag or through cheesecloth. It's easiest if you have a large bowl underneath to catch the filtered milk. Now holding the bag with one hand, squeeze out the additional milk with your other hand.

Tip: If you dehydrate the almond pulp, you can use it to make raw cakes and cookies. Many save it in the fridge for about 2 days (shake before drinking), although I prefer to drink it fresh. You can buy nut bags at most health stores and online. You can also use nylons, cheesecloth, or a paint strainer.

Chai Nut Milk

Prep: 15 minutes

   1½ teaspoons garam marsala
   1 teaspoon ground ginger
   1 teaspoon cinnamon
   ½ teaspoon ground cardamom
   ½ teaspoon nutmeg

Add the above spices to your almond milk mixture when blending in your high-speed blender. Store nut milk in a large canning jar with lid in your refrigerator. You will drink it up before it goes bad.

Chocolate Almond Milk

Prep: 10 minutes

Add 1–2 tablespoons raw cacao powder when making almond milk and blend together in high-speed blender. If you can't eat raw cacao powder, substitute carob powder. I use two tablespoons or more, as I love chocolate. If you want to add a little extra chocolate crunch to your drink, you can sprinkle it with raw cacao nibs.

Hemp Heaven

Anjou and Jaime Jones (The Date People)
Prep: 5 minutes

½ cup soft dates, pitted
½ cup hemp seeds
4 cups water

Place ingredients in a high-speed blender and blend until smooth.

As a variation, try adding your favorite fresh fruit, cacao, vanilla bean, or ice.

Soups

When you're feeling under the weather, when the dampness of fall gives way to the chill winds of winter and frost starts to creep in the air, soup is what my body calls for. People are always astonished that, as a raw foodist, I still eat soup. Keep in mind that the magic number when cooking raw (to keep it full of nutrition and enzymes) is 118°F. You can make warm soup and keep it under that magic number (although any soup close to "scalding temperatures" is going to go above 118°F).

I have a slow cooker that, when set to its low temperature, lets me include all the ingredients I want to while keeping to the criteria of temperatures below 118°F, while still slowly cooking the ingredients. First thing in the morning on a Saturday or Sunday (or better yet, the night before) I place the ingredients in the slow cooker. By the end of the day, the soup will be ready to eat.

Vegetarians and/or those who want to live a healthier life style can feel free to raise the temperature on your slow cooker, or even use a soup pot on your stovetop to make your soup. I want to encourage you to start eating and living a healthy lifestyle. Too many people think that eating healthy is hard. It *isn't* hard—but you *do* have to start. Like any change in life, one step at a time, one recipe or one dish at a time—and in this case, one soup at a time—is all it takes!

Bali Blues aka Butternut Squash Soup or East-Meets-West Soup

Prep: 11 minutes   **Cooking Time:** 8–12 hours (under 118°F)

48 ounces butternut squash, peeled and
    chopped up
2–3 (8-ounce) cans of coconut milk
1 stalk of lemongrass, peeled and
    chopped
3 carrots, chopped
3 celery stalks, chopped
¼ cup red onion, finely chopped

2 cloves, garlic chopped
1 teaspoon curry powder (or to taste)
1 teaspoon cinnamon (or to taste)
1 tablespoon raw honey
Sea salt, to taste
Ground black pepper, to taste
1 small soup bone (optional)

Place ingredients in a slow cooker and stir. Continue to stir throughout the process. When the soup has cooked long enough that you can get a fork through the butternut squash pieces, combine the squash with soup liquid in your blender and blend. I work my way through the bulk of the butternut squash and vegetables, and then pour back into the slow cooker. You can leave some of the vegetables whole so that it will have a chunky texture. If you wish the soup to be smooth, then blend all of the ingredients after cooked through in your blender until smooth and pour back into the slow cooker to meld a little bit longer. Please be sure to remove bone from soup when blending in blender. Note that if you do not include the bone in this recipe, it is considered a vegetarian recipe.

If you are wondering why this soup has so many names, it is because they all apply! When I got back from my trip to Bali, Indonesia (where pumpkin soup was abundant), I found myself already missing Bali and its warmth. I made this soup to warm me up and to remind me of my time in Bali. I refer to this as my "East-Meets-West Soup" because it includes my local staples like carrots, onion, and celery, and then Bali-inspired ingredients like lemongrass, curry, and cinnamon.

I hope you enjoy this soup as much as I enjoyed creating it and eating it. Maybe when you are eating this soup, you'll be able to picture and feel the happiness and joy that I experienced while in Bali—and ever since!

Tomato, Mushroom Vegetable Soup

Prep: 15 minute

> **2 quarts cold packed-tomatoes**
> **2 tablespoons sun dried tomatoes**
> **¼–½ cup onion, diced**
> **2 large carrots, chopped**
> **2 celery stalks, chopped**
> **1 large cup mushrooms, sliced (portabella or shitake work well)**
> **1 zucchini, thinly sliced**
> **1 yellow squash, thinly sliced**
> **2 garlic cloves, minced**
> **Seasonings to taste (sea salt, ground black pepper, Italian seasonings)**

Combine ingredients in a slow cooker. Make sure vegetables are covered with liquid. You can add another quart of cold-packed tomatoes or fresh mashed tomatoes or add additional water. Stir periodically. Cook on low temperature in a slow cooker (with the temperature low it will take a good 8–12 hours) until you can get a fork through the vegetables. Once you can get a fork through the vegetables and the soup is warm, your soup is ready to eat. Mmm . . . good. Please note that soup is best eaten in a bowl by a lit fireplace.

Asian Spice Blend

Yield: 12 teaspoons or ¼ cup

Spice Blend
2 teaspoons cinnamon
1½ tablespoons coriander
1½ tablespoons turmeric
1 teaspoon clove powder
1 teaspoon paprika
2 teaspoons powdered ginger

Noodles
1 cup mung bean sprouts
1 cup kelp noodles (rinsed and soaked to soften, then cut into 1½ to 2 inch long pieces)
1 avocado, julienned (cut in thin strips)
½ cup carrot, julienned in 1-inch long pieces (use a julienne peeler)
½ cup baby bok choy, thinly sliced strips (cut into 1-inch long pieces)
½ cup shitake mushrooms, thinly sliced
¼ cup snow peas, thinly sliced strips
¼ cup hijiki, soaked to soften (strain before adding to soup)

Noodles

Prepare vegetables and hand-fold into the soup base. Serve chilled or at room temperature. If you wish to eat your soup warm, heat it in a pot on top of the oven, checking the temperature to make sure it stays below 118°F (if you wish the soup to be considered raw).

Coconut meat can also be used for the noodles. Thinly slice (julienne) the meat of one young Thai coconut and cut strips into one inch pieces. Fold these in with the other noodles.

For a spicier soup, add 1 Thai chili pod cut in half and de-seed, or else add ⅛ teaspoon cayenne. To prepare Thai chili-pod, submerge the chili pod into the soup mixture for 5–10 minutes. Promptly remove, as the chili is very hot and will continue to carry its spice over into the mixture the longer it sits.

Asian-Thai Inspired Soup

Brenda Hinton, Rawsome Creations
Prep: 35 minutes   **Yield:** 6 cups

Broth
3–4 large stalks celery, rough-chopped (about 3 cups)
1 large cucumber, peeled and rough-chopped (about 4 cups)
2½ cups coconut water (from 2 young Thai coconuts)
3 tablespoons lemon juice
2 tablespoons fresh lemongrass, chopped (about one small lemongrass)

Soup
2 tablespoons white miso
½ teaspoon Asian Spice Blend (See recipe on page 132)

Broth
Add ingredients to a high-speed blender and blend until smooth, about one minute. Place "More than a Nut Milk Bag" over a large pitcher and strain blended mixture through one or two bags. Return broth to the blender once strained.

Soup
Add to the broth and blend until spices are fully incorporated. If you remove the miso the recipe would then be considered raw.

Sweet Corn Chowder

Brenda Hinton, Rawsome Creations
Yield: 5 cups   **Prep:** 25 minutes

6 cups of sweet corn, divided into two equal portions
1 cup almond milk
2 tablespoons lime juice
2 teaspoons white miso
1 teaspoon fresh garlic (1 large clove)
1 tablespoon Red Star nutritional yeast
1 teaspoon cumin
1 teaspoon sea salt
⅛ teaspoon jalapeño chili powder
¼ cup minced red onion

In a high-speed blender, combine 3 cups corn, almond milk, lime juice, white miso, garlic, nutritional yeast, cumin, jalapeño powder, and salt. Blend until mixture is smooth.

Transfer mixture to a mixing bowl and gently fold in the remaining 3 cups of corn and the minced onion. Garnish with chili flakes and freshly ground pepper. Served chilled, at room temperature or warm.

This recipe may be stored in air-tight glass containers in the refrigerator up to one week or can be frozen for up to 2 months.

Berry Refreshing Soup

Elysa Markowitz, "Living with Greenstar" (courtesy of Tribest)
Prep: 15 minutes   **Yield:** 2 servings

> 6 oranges, juiced
> 2 limes
> 1 box fresh berries (strawberries, blackberries, raspberries, or blueberries)
> Spearmint, garnish

Use the fine screen in your juicer. Juice peeled oranges and ½ lime, unpeeled. Pour fresh berries into the mixture. Serve in bowls, garnished with fresh spearmint leaves.

Sweet Limey Soup

Elysa Markowitz, "Living with Greenstar" (courtesy of Tribest)
Prep: 15 minutes   **Yield:** 4 servings

> 4 tangelos
> 4 tangerines
> 1 lime
> 1 bunch of grapes

Use the coarse screen on your Greenstar Elite Juicer. To make the broth, juice 3 peeled tangelos, 3 peeled tangerines, and ¼ of the lime (unpeeled). Slice the remaining tangelo and tangerine into the broth. Float the grapes and lime slices on top of the soup. Serve in a pretty bowl.

Island Paradise Soup

Elysa Markowitz, "Living with Greenstar" (courtesy of Tribest)
Prep: 15 minutes   **Yield:** 2 servings

    2 celery stalks
    ½ pineapple
    2 cups purple grapes
    1 cup mango puree

Use the fine screen when juicing your ingredients for this recipe. To make the broth, juice celery and peeled pineapple, leaving 2 pineapple slices for the soup. Pour mango puree in a circle around the pineapple juice, adding grapes and pineapple slices to the broth. Serve in pretty bowls.

   To make things easier, vertically slice the pineapple into long and narrow sticks so that they are easier to feed into the juicer. This will make your juicing easier. The celery gives a salty flavor so start with one piece of celery and taste. Add more celery if desired.

Peachy Keen Soup

Elysa Markowitz, "Living with Greenstar" (courtesy of Tribest)
Freezing time: 6–8 hours   **Prep:** 10 minutes   **Yield:** 2 servings

    1 box strawberries
    3 bananas
    2 peaches
    2–4 spearmint leaves

Use the blank blade on your juicer for this recipe. To make the soup broth, alternate putting 2 bananas fresh or frozen with ½ box of fresh strawberries through the machine. Pour into a bowl. Float strawberries, banana, and peach slices in the broth. Serve in a pretty bowl garnished with spearmint leaves.

Plum Good Soup

 R V GF P

Elysa Markowitz, "Living with Greenstar" (courtesy of Tribest)
Prep: 15 minutes   **Yield:** 2 servings

  4 apples
  1 lemon
  2 nectarines
  2 plums

Use the fine screen for your Greenstar Elite Juicer for this recipe. To make the broth, juice 3 apples and ¼ lemon with the rind. In a blender, finish making the broth by blending apple juice with 1 nectarine. Float plum, nectarine, and apple slices in the broth. Serve in a fancy bowl, garnished with apple and lemon slices.

  Fuji apples are the best apples to juice. If you don't have Fujis available, use a firm and crisp apple. If you find plums skin too tart, then feel free to peel it. Otherwise please enjoy the contrast of the sweet and sour.

Steamy Basil Soup

R V GF P

Elysa Markowitz, "Living with Greenstar" (courtesy of Tribest)
Prep: 25 minutes   **Yield:** 4–6 servings

  2 cups fresh carrot juice
  1 avocado
  6–10 fresh basil leaves
  1 lemon

Use the fine screen on your Tribest Greenstar Elite Juicer for this recipe. To make the broth, juice the carrots first. In a blender, mix carrot juice, avocado, and basil leaves together, spicing to taste. Serve in a lovely bowl. Garnish with lemon slices and a fresh basil leaf.

Corny Soup

Elysa Markowitz, "Living with Greenstar" (courtesy of Tribest)
Prep: 20 minutes   **Yield:** 4–6 servings

    4 cups fresh carrot juice
    1 avocado
    1–2 slices fresh ginger root
    2 ears fresh white corn
    1 lime
    Celtic sea salt

Use the fine screen on your Tribest Greenstar Elite Juicer for this recipe. To make the broth, juice the carrots, and then blend together the carrot juice, avocado, and spice with the ginger root to taste. Add the corn last and blend to desired smoothness. Serve in a pretty bowl spicing with lime juice and Celtic Sea Salt to taste. Garnish with lime and a slice of fresh ginger.

Christmas Delight Soup

R **V** **GF** **P**

Elysa Markowitz, "Living with Greenstar" (courtesy of Tribest)
Prep: 25 minutes   **Yield:** 2 servings

Broth
1 cup purple cabbage
6–8 large red tomatoes

Soup Fillings
6 fresh basil leaves
½ cup fresh parsley
1 cup green cabbage, chopped
2 limes

Use the blank screen for this recipe. To make the soup broth, alternate putting fresh red tomatoes and purple cabbage through the machine and into a bowl. Stir with a whisk to blend the flavors.

Pour water through the machine to clear out the tomato or rinse out the housing and twin gears and reassemble. Then put basil, parsley, and green cabbage through the machine and into a separate bowl.

Serve in a bowl. First pour in the red mixture and then the green mixture on top in a ring. Garnish with tomato and lime slices, with parsley and basil on top of the slices. Merry Christmas and bon appetit!

Blushing Borscht

Elysa Markowitz, "Living with Greenstar" (courtesy of Tribest)

Prep: 25 minutes   **Yield:** 4–6 servings

Broth
2 cups carrot juice (8–10 carrots)
½ cup beet juice (2–3 beets)
¼ cup apple juice (3–5 apples)
1 lemon

Soup Fillings
1 cup fresh dill weed
2 green onions
2 beets
1 cup purple cabbage, finely chopped
1 carrot

Topping
1 avocado
1 celery stalk

1 lemon
Celtic sea salt

Please use the fine screen on your juicer for this recipe. To make the broth, juice the carrots, beets, apples, and ¼ lemon with peel. In a blender, mix dill weed, 1 green onion with broth, spicing with Celtic sea salt and lemon juice to taste. Put finely grated beets, carrot, and cabbage into the broth, adding finely chopped dill weed last. To make the toppings, in a blender blend avocado, 1 green onion, and celery, seasoning with lemon juice and Celtic sea salt to taste.

Garnish soup with topping and fresh dill.

Asparagus Soup

Elysa Markowitz, courtesy of Tribest

Prep: 25 minutes   **Yield:** 4 servings

Broth
6–8 red tomatoes, large
4–6 dried tomatoes
1 bunch asparagus (save tips as garnish)
4–8 fresh basil leaves

Soup Fillings
4–6 yellow tomatoes
1 lime
½ cup fresh parsley

Use the blank screen on your juicer for this recipe. To make the soup broth, alternate putting fresh red tomatoes and dried tomatoes, basil, and asparagus stalks (save the tips) through the machine, into a bowl. Stir with a whisk to blend the flavors. Save one red and one yellow tomato for garnishing.

To clear out the red tomato, pour water through the machine or rinse the housing and twin gears and reassemble. Then put the yellow tomatoes through the machine and put into a separate bowl.

Serve into soup bowls. Place a slice of lime in each bowl and pour in the red mixture followed by the yellow mixture around the top in a ring. Garnish with lime, basil, parsley, red and yellow tomato slices, and raw asparagus tips.

Chunky Veggie Soup

Elysa Markowitz, courtesy of Tribest

Prep: 25 minutes   **Yield:** 4–6 servings

Broth
2–2½ cups carrot juice
1 avocado
4–6 celery stalks
1 lemon

Soup Fillings
1 summer squash
2 carrots
2–3 ears fresh corn
2–4 celery stalks
1 cup arugula
Slice options: parsley, basil, or cilantro

Use the fine screen on your juicer for this recipe.

To make the broth, simply juice the carrots.

In a blender, mix carrot juice, avocado, 3–4 celery stalks (to taste), spicing with lemon juicer after it is blended smoothly. Add finely grated squash, carrots, and corn (cut off the cob) with finely diced celery and finely chopped arugula. Add other fresh green herbs last. Serve in a pretty bowl or cup. Garnish with lemon slices and fresh herbs.

Raw Veg Soup

Courtesy of Vitamix

Prep: 10 minutes   **Yield:** 400 milliliters

100 milliliters cold water
Juice of ½ lime
60 milliliters unsweetened almond milk
1 avocado, very ripe, halved and stoned
1½ teaspoon soy sauce or wheatfree tamari
1–2 drops Tabasco Sauce
1.5 centimeter piece fresh ginger, peeled
100 grams celery
25 grams spinach
60 grams carrot (or 1 large carrot)

Place all ingredients into the Vitamix 64-ounce container in the order listed and secure lid. Turn the dial to 1 and slowly increase speed to 10. Blend for 45 seconds. Serve with ice cubes, a drop or two of toasted sesame oil, and some coriander leaves.

African Sweet Potato–Peanut Soup

Sheryll Chavarria
Yield: 8–10 servings

¼ cup coconut oil
2 large onions, chopped
3-4 cloves garlic, minced
1 tablespoon minced fresh ginger root
1 tablespoon ground cumin
½–1 teaspoon ground cinnamon
½ teaspoon ground cloves
8 medium tomatoes, chopped
4 medium sweet potatoes, peeled and chopped
3 carrots, peeled and chopped
2 cups chopped, unsalted dry-roasted peanuts
1 cup creamy peanut butter
10 cups water
Pinch cayenne pepper (optional)
Chopped fresh cilantro as garnish
Salt, to taste

Heat the oil in a large saucepan over medium–high heat. Sauté the onions for 10 minutes, until lightly browned. Mix in the garlic, ginger, cumin, cinnamon, and cloves. Stir in the tomatoes, sweet potatoes, and carrot and continue to cook and stir for about 5 minutes.

Pour water into the saucepan, and season the mixture with salt. Bring to a boil, reduce heat, and simmer for 30 minutes.

Remove the soup mixture from heat. In a food processor or blender, blend the soup and peanuts until almost smooth. Season with cayenne pepper. Return to the saucepan. Whisk in the peanut butter, and cook until heated through. Serve warm topped with fresh cilantro.

Minestrone

Brenda Hinton, Rawsome Creations

Prep: 30 minutes   **Yield:** 6 cups

3 large Roma tomatoes, rough-chopped
2 cups orange juice (about 2 medium oranges)
1 teaspoon salt
1 teaspoon coriander
1 teaspoon cumin
1 teaspoon onion powder
4 teaspoons tomato powder
½ cup zucchini, finely diced
½ cup Roma tomato, finely diced
½ cup carrot, finely diced
½ cup celery, finely diced
½ cup corn kernels
½ cup peas
½ cup broccoli florets finely cut (optional)

Peel the oranges, cutting away the pith and rind. Rough-chop peeled oranges and tomatoes and place in a high-speed blender. Blend until smooth or about approximately 30–40 seconds. Strain blended mixture through Rawsome Creation's "More Than a Nut Milk Bag" and catch resulting juice in a mixing bowl. This produces about four cups of juice. Set aside.

Whisk in salt, coriander, cumin, onion powder, and tomato powder. Finally, fold in the remaining vegetables. Serve chilled or at room temperature, or else heat it up, making sure temperature stays below 118°F if you wish the soup to be considered raw.

Bolivian Creamy Quinoa Peanut Soup (Sopa De Mani)

Sheryll Chavarria
Yield: 8–10 servings

¼ cup coconut oil
2 cloves garlic, pressed
2 medium onions, medium chopped
1 tablespoon cumin
1 tablespoon oregano
2 cups raw white peanuts (blended with water, keep a little chunky)
¼ bunch parsley, chopped
½ bag frozen peas
1 cup chopped green beans (cut off ends)
3 cups chopped red bliss potatoes
½ cup brown rice
½ cup quinoa
Salt, to taste

Fry garlic and onions in coconut oil. Add salt, cumin, and oregano, and then add peanut puree. Fill pot about half way with water and cook for about half hour. Add all the rest of the ingredients and cook for another 20 minutes to a half an hour.

Water
and Teas

WATER

Water makes up not only most of our planet, but most of our bodies as well. Over 70 percent of our body is made up of water, which it uses like an engine uses fuel. We use water to keep our body temperature regulated, we use it to eliminate wastes from our body, and we use it to clean and restore the outside of our body.

So it should come as no surprise that the quality of the water we drink is paramount to achieving excellent health. Our body's inner workings are intricate, and it's amazing how well it works, even when we abuse it—whether through lack of sleep, toxic food, or a toxic environment (be it toxic people or pollutants).

When speaking with a doctor (an attending physician during one of my mom's hospital stays), he told me that we were divinely created in such a way that our organs have excess capacity. What that means is that by the time we start to have issues, we have already *over*-abused our bodies. If something as simple as drinking enough water a day and making sure the water is pure and healthy can keep our bodies working like a well-oiled machine, then why not do it?

Believe it or not, some folks don't like drinking water and don't allow it any place in their diet. A great way to add extra flavor and healing to your water—while making it more attractive to those unused to enjoying water—is by infusing (adding) ingredients (such as fruit) to your waters.

I never really drank tea while growing up. I didn't much care for the taste; it's the same reason I never got into drinking coffee. But when taking my Homesteads Herbalism course at Farm At Coventry, as well as classes at Nettlejuice Herbals and my Permaculture course at Permanent Future, I learned how drinking herbal teas can be a great way of naturally addressing body issues. I think my favorite is drinking dried catnip tea—it's great for stomachaches. What used to be a ho—hum plain cup of tea becomes a cup of healing that tastes fabulous. Adding different ingredients to your tea (I've shared a few recipes below) is like creating your own personal, all-natural medicine chest that you can easily ingest by drinking. Not only are these teas great for you, but they end up tasting great!

Chickweed Tea

Add 1–2 teaspoon of the dried herb to 8 ounces of water. Steep (covered) 20 minutes. Drink up to 3 cups a day.

Chickweed is abundant in vitamins and minerals, strengthens your systems, is good at dissolving, *and* helpful in losing weight.

Nettle Tea

Add 2 teaspoons of the dried herb to 8 ounces water. Steep for 30 minutes. Drink 1–3 cups per day.

Nettle tea is rich in minerals and is a great blood cleanser. Drinking nettle tea will improve the health and function of the body systems and increase overall health and vitality. It is also a diuretic and an anti-arthritic.

Nettle leaves are great in soups, pâtés, and drinks. Remember that nettles sting, so wear gloves when cutting them and use tongs to avoid touching them. If you don't want to grow it, you can always buy it.

Dandelion Root Tea

V **GF** **P**

Add 2 teaspoon of freshly dried root to 8 ounces water. Decoct for 20 minutes. Drink 3 cups per day.

Dandelion root tea acts as a digestive tonic, mild laxative, and diuretic. It's great for your liver, helps with sluggish bowels and chronic constipation, and stimulates the growth of healthy bowel flora.

When we were growing up, my mom would pay us a penny a piece to pull out dandelions in our yard, as she considered them a weed. I didn't know how good they were for us until I started taking my herbalism classes. In addition to the root, you can also eat the dandelion flower and leaves.

Ginger Tea

V **GF** **P**

Add 1.2 teaspoon to 8 ounces of water. Steep and cover for 20 minutes. Drink 2–3 cups per day.

Not only is ginger a great seasoning for our food, but it's good for an upset stomach. I always take ginger tablets with me when I travel on a plane or boat, as it works well for motion sickness. It also helps with nausea, morning sickness, and upset stomachs caused by chemotherapy.

Holy Basil Tea

V **GF** **P**

Add 1 teaspoon dried leaf to 8 ounces of water. Steep for 20 minutes. Drink 3 cups per day.

Holy basil strengthens the immune system and aids the body with physical stamina. It also assists in digestion and helps the body absorb the nutrients from food. It can support the function of the heart, lungs, and liver, increase circulation and memory, and is often used to promote clear thinking and focus. Holy basil tea can also stimulate the pituitary and immune systems.

Lavender Tea

Add ¼–½ teaspoon dried lavender to 8 ounces of water. Steep covered for 15–20 minutes. Drink 4 ounces, 2–3 times a day.

We all know that lavender smells nice and is used in soaps and herbal pillows for its soothing and antidepressant qualities. But did you know it's also good for gas and nausea? Lavender is antiseptic and can kill abnormal bacteria in the bowels. You can combine lavender with a probiotic for best results. You can also combine lavender with ginger for travel sickness.

Catnip Tea

Add 1–2 teaspoons dried herb to 8 ounces of water. Steep, covered, for 20 minutes. Drink up to 3–4 cups a day.

In addition to making your cats happy, catnip is good for stomach aches, flus, and colds.

Peppermint Tea

Add 1–2 teaspoon dried herb to 8 ounces water. Steep for 5–15 minutes. Drink up to 3–4 cups a day.

Peppermint makes food taste good and your breath smell nice. It is also good for nausea, gas, and stomach challenges, as well as cold and flu fevers.

Rose Tea

Add 1–2 teaspoons dried petals to 8 ounces of water. Steep covered for 20 minutes.

I love the rose. Not only is it good for your heart (if you are grieving from heartache or loss) but rose petals and hips served as a tea can bring down fevers and clear toxins from the body. The hips contain Vitamin C.

Never use roses from the florist. Make sure the roses you use are chemical, pesticide, and preservative free. As with anything, if you don't know where or what soil the plant was grown in, do not ingest it or use on your body.

Lemonade

Add your steeped herbs to your favorite freshly squeezed lemon, water, and raw honey. Stir, cool, and drink.

Not everyone likes teas, so another way to drink your healthy herbs is in a lemonade concoction. The lemon will cover up the taste of the herbs, in case you don't like the taste of the herbs themselves.

Jamu: A Turmeric Tonic

Brenda Hinton, Rawsome Creations
Yield: 16 ounces   **Prep:** 10 minutes

6–7 inches thumb-sized fresh turmeric root
6–7 inches, thumb-sized fresh ginger root

2 lemons, peeled
8 ounces water
2 teaspoons agave, honey, maple syrup (or other liquid sweetener)

Juicer Version

Juice the ginger, turmeric, and lemons to yield approximately 8 ounces of liquid. Add the water and honey, stirring to combine all ingredients.

Blender Version

Cut peeled lemons into quarters and place in a blender. Chop turmeric and ginger root into smaller ½-inch pieces. Add these to the blender and blend until completely smooth. It may be necessary to use a small amount of water. Squeeze pulp mixture through a "More Than a Nut Milk Bag" (www.rawsomecreations.com) for approximately 8 ounces of liquid. Add water and honey to this liquid, stirring to combine all ingredients.

Your tonic can be stored in a glass jar in the refrigerator for several days.

Turmeric juice can stain everything a sort of yellow/orange color, including your hands, so it is best to use gloves when squeezing through a nut milk bag. It is also best to use glass, stainless steel, or dark colors for spatulas, bowls, or storage containers.

My love affair with Bali began long before, while thinking about my product line for Rawsome Creations (www.rawsomecreations.com). Now that I travel to this magical island on a regular basis, I have come to know and appreciate the herbal remedies and culinary magic of the traditional Balinese people. I discovered Jamu on one of my first visits. This dark yellow-orange colored tonic—often called Indonesia's cure-all elixir—is commonly made in household kitchens and cafes throughout Bali. The simple primary ingredients of turmeric root and lemon juice (mixed with honey) form a powerful medicinal tonic. Adding ginger to this wonder juice can help as an anti-inflammatory, liver detoxifier, and kidney cleanser while warming the body and improving circulation.

This recipe is inspired by Ibu Rika.

Water Infusions

Regardless of whether you have a fancy Takeya Flash Chill Iced Tea Maker with a fruit infuser, if you want to drink water that has been infused with fruit, herbs, or vegetables, it is very simple: If you don't have an infuser available, freeze your fruit and drop it into your pitcher, glass, or bottle of water. It's really very simple. Not only does it taste good and look pretty, it's good for you, too.

In addition to water and ice, I will typically add:

- Strawberries
- Lemons
- Cucumbers
- Mint
- Fresh herbs
- Orange slices
- Lemon slices
- Grapes
- Blueberries
- Watermelon chunks
- Lime slices

You can use either fresh or frozen fruit when preparing your infusions. Remember that you can be creative; you don't need to follow my above suggestions. Likewise, you can go crazy and use *all* of the above! It's up to you; you are limited only by your imagination. These drinks are refreshing and all natural, and you don't have to worry about reading a package to see what the contents are—you know what they are, and that they are clean, fresh, and good for you.

These drinks really jazz up the beverage portion of your refreshments; your guests will think you spent hours preparing the drinks! This in turn will make your guests feel extra special.

Coconut Milk and Coconut Water

Prep: 5 minutes

1 young Thai Coconut

Use the back end of a cleaver knife and cut a circle around the top of the coconut. To make coconut water, simply pour the liquid out from the young Thai coconut after opening and drink.

For coconut milk, blend the coconut water and the meat (which you can remove from the inside of the coconut using an ice cream scoop) and combine them together in a high-speed blender.

Water Kefir: A Dairy-Free Probiotic Beverage

Melissa Miles (Permanent Future Institute)
Prep: 10 minutes

> **6 cups water, brought just to a boil**
> **¼ cup organic sugar**
> **¼ cup water kefir grains**
> **2 quart jar**
> **½ organic lemon (optional)**
> **Handful unsulphured dried fruit (optional)**

Bring water just to a boil, before turning off heat and stirring in the ¼ cup organic sugar until it is dissolved. Allow mixture to cool to room temperature. Place ¼ cup water kefir grains into a 2 quart jar. Pour in the cooled sugar water. Optionally, you can drop in a handful of unsulphured dried fruit and ½ organic lemon.

Cover the jar loosely with lid or with cheesecloth. Secure with a rubber band to allow air in but prevent bugs from entering the jar. Ferment out of direct sunlight at room temperature for 2–3 days. The longer it ferments, the stronger the flavor. When the desired flavor is reached, strain it through a nonreactive (plastic, wood, or stainless steel) strainer into another 2-quart jar. Leave some head space (discard the spent lemon and dried fruit), but reserve the water kefir grains. Enjoy your water kefir beverage immediately or store in refrigerator.

Alternatively, you can try a secondary ferment to add more flavor to the brew: Pour either ¼ cup fruit juice of your choice or 1 tablespoon organic cane sugar into flip-top bottles. Pour the water kefir from the 2-quart jar into bottles, filling them up to within 1 inch of the opening. Seal the bottles and set them on a countertop to ferment for an additional 18–24 hours (keeping in mind that warm temperatures will speed up the fermentation process, and cool temperatures will slow it down). Grains can be immediately re-cultured or stored in water in the fridge for a few weeks, or frozen or dehydrated for longer storage.

Probiotics aid you in digesting food, particularly hard-to-digest foods and foods to which some individuals are more sensitive. They enhance the synthesis of B vitamins and improve calcium absorption. They also help to keep a healthy balance of intestinal microflora.

Basic Kombucha

Melissa Miles (Permanent Future Institute)
Prep: 10–15 minutes

> 3 quarts non-chlorinated/filtered spring water or distilled water
> 5–7 tea bags
> ½ cup cane sugar
> 1 kombucha SCOBY (Symbiotic Culture of friendly Bacteria and Yeast)

In a large non-aluminum pot, bring water to a simmer. Note that a rolling boil will reduce oxygen and carbon, which are necessary for proper fermentation; therefore simmer, and don't boil. Add tea bags. Tea is the herb that the bacteria feeds on, so organic black or green teas are best. Steep for 5–10 minutes. Add ½ cup organic cane sugar, ½ cup white sugar (white sugar is essential to the kombucha's survival, and no substitutions should be made). Stir with wooden spoon only; ferments hate metal. Allow to cool to room temperature. Keep covered to avoid contamination.

Pour cold liquid into fermenting container (glass is best; no plastic or metal). Add kombucha SCOBY with 2 cups of previously fermented starter. (If none are available, use ¼ cup white distilled vinegar to reduce the pH and protect against all pathogens. Do not use unpasteurized non-distilled apple cider vinegar.)

Cover with a clean cloth. Set aside in an undisturbed spot out of direct sunlight to ferment. Ferment for 6–8 days at a constant temperature of 75–80°F. You should notice an apple cider aroma when finished. If you notice any mold or unpleasant smell, discard the entire batch, SCOBY and all (you cannot salvage a moldy SCOBY).

To bottle, choose a glass container (from which you will need to consume the entire amount within 1–2 days; otherwise, you'll risk having the tea turn flat). You may choose to filter the tea through cheesecloth. While this may filter possible contaminants, it also reduces some beneficial bacteria and the taste becomes lighter. I do not filter my liquid, but it is your choice. The bottled tea may be left on the counter at room temperature to allow for an additional 2–3 days of fermentation. Refrigerate the final brew.

Note that kombucha has been known to "contaminate" other ferments, so keep it away from sourdough, kefir, lacto-ferments, and so on. Raw foodists and the health world are really into kombucha and kefirs because of their many health benefits.

Coconut Water Kefir

Melissa Miles (Permanent Future Institute)
Prep: 10–15 minutes

   4 cups young coconut water
   4 tablespoons water kefir grains

Combine the coconut water and the grains in a jar and let set for 12–24 hours. Some people like to add a tablespoon of organic cane sugar, but this is optional. Coconut water tends to ferment quickly and the flavor will become more intense (sour and tangy). Taste often; when you are satisfied with the result, just strain the grains out and enjoy. Grains can be stored in refrigerator or start another batch right away.

Green Tea Citrus Drink

Prep: 15 minutes   **Yield:** 1650 milliliters

   300 milliliters green tea with lemon
   150 milliliters pear juice
   1 orange, peeled, quartered
   1 lemon, peeled, halved
   1 lime, peeled, halved
   1½ pear, seeded, rough cut
   2½ tablespoons honey
   ¾ tablespoon ground cinnamon
   3 sprigs lemon balm, picked
   375 grams ice cubes

Place all ingredients into the high-speed blender container in the order listed and secure lid. Select Variable 1. Turn machine on and slowly increase speed to Variable 10, then High. Blend for 45 seconds.

Conclusion

"Success doesn't come to you, you go to it."
—ANONYMOUS

Just as success won't come to you unless you go to it, living a healthy, vibrant and dynamic life doesn't happen by chance—it happens by setting goals, planning for success, a lot of prayer, and the will to make it happen. *Liquid Health* was written first and foremost to serve as a tool to help you live a healthy lifestyle and support your choice to live your life dynamically.

"Do not go where the path may lead, go instead where there is no path and leave a trail."
—RALPH WALDO EMERSON

As we go through the ups and downs of life, it can seem as though the downs are impossible to get through. Sometimes it seems like you walk through the fires alone, and that no one has it as bad as you. Know that you will make it through, even if you can't quite see the light at the end of the tunnel. Those same fires you walk through are refining fire, a crucible to strengthen and empower us. Think back: remember all of the horrific times in your life. You got through each and every one of them to stand here today. That's why I wrote *Liquid Health*; I want it to support you during those ups and downs of life, so that you can thrive every day.

Acknowledgments

A very special thank you to all those who have made this book possible. Thank you to Martin Pearl and Hatherleigh Press; thank you to all of the contributors; thank you to the ones who taught us, loved us, stood alongside us, and supported us throughout the years!

Also, a very special *thank you* to *you,* the reader; you who have touched my life, and helped to bring *Liquid Health* to fruition.

And finally, a thank you to the challenges of life which have given us the opportunity to learn, grow, and "live dynamically!"

I pray that *Liquid Health* will inspire you, support you, and help you to become the best that you can be!

Many thanks,
Lisa

Resources

HORIZON HERBS

Williams, Oregon
(541) 846-6704
www.horizonherbs.com
Besides browsing their inventory online and purchasing through their website, you can also get on their mailing list, which will allow you to receive their catalog—containing native medicinal seeds and plants of the world.

KING'S HERB NOOK

Honey Brook, Pennsylvania
(610) 273-4583
If you don't have the space and/or time to grow and dry your own tea ingredients, you can purchase them at King's Herb Nook. In addition to dried ingredients, they sell fresh herbs in season and sponsor an assortment of healthy herbal classes. I always buy more than I plan to!

LORETA'S LIVING FOOD

Malvern, Pennsylvania
Loreta's Living Food has been growing wheatgrass and sprouts for over 25 years. Loreta was my first raw teacher, and she still holds workshops today. If you have the opportunity, I definitely recommend that you try Loreta's wheatgrass (pre-cut), sprouts and workshops.

MOUNTAIN ROSE HERBS

Eugene, Oregon
(800) 879-3337
Mountain Rose Herbs has a large website and catalog available, allowing you to purchase native medicinal seeds and plants. If you aren't in a position where you have the time or space to grow and utilize your own weeds or herbs, and don't have the luxury of a permaculture or herbalist teacher, you can purchase dried

herbs at their website or via their catalog. You can also have the option to buy in bulk.

SPROUTMAN'S WHEATGRASS

I often buy Sproutman's Wheatgrass (by the tray) at my local health food market. When I get the tray home, I cut it off of the mat and place the cut wheatgrass in a ziplock bag (with paper towels to absorb any moistness). Don't make the same mistake I did the first time I bought the wheatgrass by the tray: I left the wheatgrass on the mat, thinking it would last longer. Instead, it turned yellow and disgusting.

Fun fact: in the summer months, you can take the mat (once it's been cut) and put it outside, and you will get a second growing. It won't be as potent as the first cutting, but when you're pinching pennies, a second growing is a viable option.

Recipe Index

NOTES

NOTES

NOTES

NOTES

NOTES

NOTES

NOTES

NOTES

NOTES

NOTES

NOTES

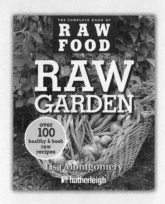
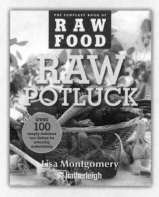

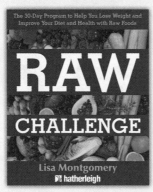